THE KENNEDY
SCANDALS & TRAGEDIES

by Ann James

PUBLICATIONS INTERNATIONAL, LTD.

Ann James is a reporter for a Boston newspaper and is a freelance writer.

CONTENTS

THE PATRIARCH: JOSEPH PATRICK KENNEDY

America's dominant political family: From left to right are Rose, Edward, Rosemary, Joseph Jr., Joseph, Eunice, Jean, John, Patricia, Robert, and Kathleen. The formal portrait was taken in London in 1939 while Joe Kennedy was ambassador to the Court of St. James's.

The Making of a Fortune

During the shady and unregulated 1920s, Kennedy was able to move stocks up and down artificially to his own benefit and that of his cronies.

Joseph Kennedy in 1945, smiling with success. The family patriarch amassed the family fortune in a number of business enterprises. None of his offspring was able to match his business acumen to increase the fortune—they were encouraged to excel in the world of politics.

The Kennedy legacy of tragedy and scandal began with Joseph Patrick Kennedy, a hard-working and hard-playing Irish American who was born in 1889.

A self-made man, Joe Kennedy reaped his fortune as a controversial investor and banker. He later turned his attention to a myriad of different activities, including filmmaking in Hollywood and international shipping. Some evidence suggests that Kennedy was even a cutthroat bootlegger during Prohibition.

As a young man in 1922, Kennedy made his first big score on the stock market after receiving an inside tip. Galen Stone, the head of a Boston financial house where the 33-year-old Kennedy worked, let his young employee in on a big secret. Stone, who was also the principal stockholder of a Kentucky coal company, was secretly negotiating with automobile giant Henry Ford to merge the company into the automobile operation. Kennedy invested heavily in the coal company. Weeks later, an announcement of the merger was made, and the coal company's stock soared. Kennedy, who had invested $24,000, suddenly found himself with a profit in excess of $435,000, a monumental sum at the time.

But it wasn't until Joe Kennedy went to New York that his prowess as a financial shark truly developed. During the shady and unregulated 1920s, Kennedy was able to move stocks up and down artificially to his own benefit and that of his cronies.

A prime example of this occurred when Kennedy agreed to help John Hertz rescue his Chicago-based Yellow Cab Company. Stock raiders were driving the company's value down until Kennedy stepped in. Backed by millions in Hertz cash, Kennedy spent a month driving the price of the stock up and down by making wild purchases from brokers across the country. The strategy worked. Eventually, the price of the cab company's stock stabilized at a very attractive price.

By the time he was 35, Kennedy was a millionaire many times over.

Ironically, President Franklin Roosevelt appointed Joe Kennedy in 1934 as the first chairman of the Securities and Exchange Commission, a new agency designed to curb the same wild and unscrupulous stock dealings of the 1920s that helped Kennedy make his millions.

The scene on Wall Street (left) was chaotic on the day the stock market crashed in 1929. Joe Kennedy was able to manipulate the stock market during the heady 1920s to the benefit of himself and his cronies. Ironically, Kennedy was appointed the first chairman of the federal Securities and Exchange Commission in 1934. Later, FDR became disenchanted with Kennedy, who was vocal in his support for British Prime Minister Neville Chamberlain's appeasement of Hitler at Munich. Kennedy thought Britain's entry into World War II spelled disaster. He made a nationwide radio speech (below) in January 1941 urging the United States to stay out of the war.

Rose

The Kennedy family was founded with the marriage of Rose Elizabeth Fitzgerald and Joseph Patrick Kennedy in 1914. It was a marriage that would produce nine children, including a United States president and three United States senators, and generations of pain and controversy.

Rose was the daughter of colorful Boston Mayor John J. "Honey Fitz" Fitzgerald. In a city social scene dominated by WASPs, the mayor was determined to groom his Irish-American daughter into a social climber. She was sent to the best Catholic schools in the United States and Europe.

Because both Rose and Joe came from politically active Irish families in Boston, politics was a tradition they would pass along to their sons.

Almost immediately after returning from their honeymoon, Rose was expecting their first child. The pregnancy set the tone for the next decades of their lives. Rose, the prim and proper mother, stayed in Massachusetts raising the children. Joe, meanwhile, traveled the country and the world creating the family's eventual fortune.

A harsh disciplinarian, Rose kept a tight rein on her children, organizing their time down to the minute. She went to church services almost daily and often brought the children with her. She disciplined the children with a swift whack of a ruler.

Rose Kennedy has seen a long lifetime of tragedies. Her oldest daughter was born mildly retarded. Four of her children died at young ages. The first to die was Joe Junior, the oldest child, who was killed at 29 during a dangerous mission while serving in World War II. Daughter Kathleen died in a plane crash at the age of 28. President John was killed by an assassin at the age of 46. And Robert was also slain by the bullet of an assassin while campaigning for the presidency five years after his brother's death. Rose has lived to see her grandson David die of an overdose of drugs.

In 1991, she celebrated her 101st birthday.

Rose and Joe (above) *after their 1914 wedding ceremony. The young couple were the children of Boston political rivals. Rose brought up a brood of nine Kennedy children* (opposite, top); *this jovial summer photograph was taken before Ted's birth. After Rosemary Kennedy was reported missing in Chicago in 1975, this 1940 picture of her* (opposite, bottom) *was widely circulated.*

Rosemary—She "Wasn't Quite Right"

All the Kennedy children were expected to excel in school, politics, and sports—but one child didn't fit the mold. Rosemary, born in 1918, was mildly retarded. During her childhood, the family hired special nurses and tutors in a vain attempt to make the oldest daughter more like her siblings. As Rosemary matured physically, her mood swings became more violent and frightening.

In 1941, without telling his wife, Joe arranged for Rosemary to undergo a lobotomy. The procedure was extremely experimental—some medical experts of the day held out hope the procedure would work wonders, but others worried about its long-term side effects. For Rosemary, the operation was a disaster, leaving her profoundly retarded and slightly paralyzed on her left side.

The family quietly sent her off to St. Coletta's in Wisconsin, a Catholic home for the mentally retarded. She remains there today, where she is sometimes visited by her sister Eunice. According to Kennedy biographer Doris Kearns Goodwin, Joe did not tell his wife of the lobotomy until 1961.

The Tinsel Lure of Hollywood

Sex goddess Gloria Swanson (left and below) *was too much for the philandering Kennedy to resist. She detailed their romance in her autobiography,* Swanson on Swanson. *Kennedy carried on his affairs in full view of his family. Here, Rose and Joe (opposite) are shown on their arrival in England with five of their children.*

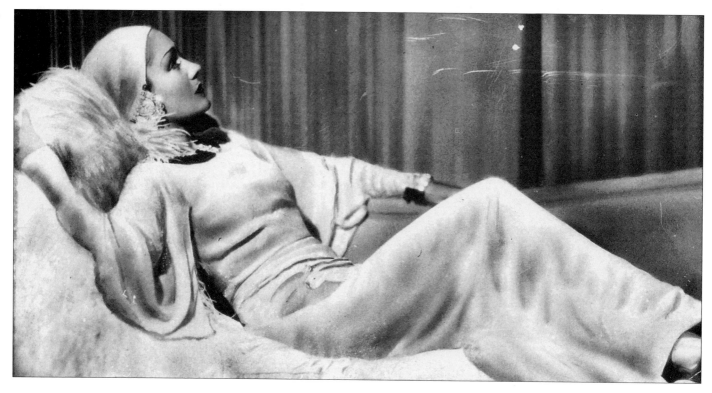

Kennedy was a feisty, energetic man, and any one venture frequently bored him. And in the late 1920s, as the stock market began to fizzle, Kennedy began to show an interest in Hollywood and filmmaking. Eventually he became one of the country's biggest film producers.

Joe Kennedy's ventures in Hollywood also produced a steamy and controversial affair: his not-so-subtle relationship with actress Gloria Swanson.

Swanson, the sex goddess of her time, quickly hit it off with Kennedy. The fact that both were married did little to stop their affair. In fact, Joe Kennedy worked hard to involve Swanson with his family. A visit she paid to the Kennedy family summer home in Hyannis Port was a town event that was heavily covered by the media. And Swanson even traveled to Europe with Joe and his wife, Rose. The two women who shared Kennedy treated each other kindly and even shopped together.

Swanson was attracted by Kennedy's financial wizardry and desired her own production house. Kennedy was infatuated with the most desirable woman of his time.

Kennedy's appetite for women never waned and was talked about frequently by his sons, who would later

share similar desires. Future President John F. Kennedy, Joe's second son, frequently shared locker-room stories about his dad's sexual exploits. According to *The Kennedys: An American Drama,* he even warned women visitors to the family's home to lock their bedroom doors because his father had "a tendency to prowl late at night."

While Joe Kennedy was womanizing and traveling the country and world amassing his family's fortune, his wife Rose stayed in Massachusetts and raised their nine children. Rose was a harsh disciplinarian who tolerated her husband's affairs in order to keep the family together.

In 1937, Joe was appointed as the United States ambassador to the Court of St. James's in England. The entire family, except for Harvard students Joe Junior and Jack, moved to England, where they were warmly received. For the rest of his life, Joe preferred to be called "ambassador."

Joe Kennedy suffered a severe stroke in 1961. It left him physically debilitated, and after a long period as a helpless invalid, he died in 1969. He had seen one son killed in war, two assassinated, and the fourth son central to the scandal of Chappaquiddick.

PT-109: Creating a Hero

World War II was the backdrop for a tragic accident that was eventually painted as a heroic rescue by Jack Kennedy.

Jack served a stint with Navy intelligence before he was given command of PT-109 in the Solomon Islands. On August 1, 1943, the patrol boat was on a mission to intercept a Japanese convoy. A Japanese destroyer, the *Amagiri,* approached the small PT boat. If the crew had been at their stations in a state of readiness, they might have seen the destroyer; if all its engines had been in gear, the patrol boat might have been able to move out of the way. Contrary to PT-boat operating procedure

in a combat zone, only one of the boat's engines was in gear. In any case, the destroyer collided with the smaller boat, ripping it in half. Two of the crew were killed, but 11, including Kennedy, survived.

As commander of the PT boat, Kennedy bore the responsibility for the boat's state of unreadiness. Once the accident had happened, he worked hard to rescue his remaining crew. He swam more than three miles to the shore of a tiny island, towing an injured crew member. Kennedy organized rescue efforts from the island and swam for hours looking in vain for American ships. Finally, after Kennedy scrawled a message on a coconut shell and gave it to island natives, an American ship rescued the men from the island.

Though having lost his ship reflected poorly on his command abilities, Kennedy's actions in saving his men were treated as heroism in news accounts of the event. Joe Kennedy made sure that a favorable article about the PT-109 incident was reprinted in *Reader's Digest,* whose large circulation ensured the widest possible exposure. The whole incident was later recounted in a book and movie, and it became a piece of American folklore.

World War II found Jack and Joe (opposite, top) *placed in danger. Putting the right spin on Jack's episode with PT-109* (opposite, bottom) *turned it into a heroic story. Jack returned alive from active duty in the Pacific; he was 26 years old* (right)*. But the eldest son, Joe* (below)*, was killed after his plane exploded on a secret mission.*

The Death of the Eldest Son

Jack's elder brother, meanwhile, was flying missions from Britain. Joe Junior was the strapping, thick-boned oldest child of the Kennedy clan. Athletic, strong-willed, and good-looking, Joe Junior often served as a father figure to his younger siblings.

During the spring of 1944, 29-year-old Joe was flying routine missions in the area of the English Channel. After serving his tour of duty, Kennedy volunteered to extend his service and fly a dangerous, top-secret mission. After the success of D-Day, Britain was under siege from the unmanned Nazi V-1 rockets. The rockets plunged British morale and killed at least 2,500 people.

Desperate to stop the bombings, the Allies conceived a plan to drop a massive bomb on the V-1 launch sites. The bomb was actually a gutted plane that was loaded with explosives. The self-assured and keenly competitive Joe Junior, who had spent his life proving he was the best at anything he did, volunteered to fly the plane.

The plan called for Kennedy and his copilot to guide the plane into the air from England. After getting the plane airborne and leaving it on autopilot, the two men would parachute from the loaded drone and the plane would be guided to the rocket site by a remote control on a nearby plane.

"I am going to do something different for the next three weeks," Joe wrote to his parents on July 26, 1944, only days before the flight. "It is secret and I am not allowed to say what it is, but it isn't dangerous, so don't worry."

But the mission was dangerous. Military historians say that the explosives inside this plane represented the largest payload ever loaded onto one plane. The plane was a PB4Y, nicknamed the Zootsuit Black. On August 12, Joe Junior guided the plane gently into the air. Only moments before he was to parachute to safety, the plane exploded prematurely in a terrific blast.

Joe Junior was killed instantly. The death hit hard in Hyannis Port, where two priests delivered the bad news to the family.

The Death of the Beautiful Young Daughter

The post–World War II era brought more heartbreak to the Kennedy family.

Kathleen Kennedy, the fourth child, had lost her husband in the war. William Cavendish, the Marquess of Hartington, had been killed by a single bullet from a German sniper during fighting in France.

Years later, Kathleen fell in love with Lord Peter Fitzwilliam. Joe and Rose strongly opposed the romance because Fitzwilliam was both Protestant and married. In 1948, however, Kathleen—who was known as Kick—convinced her father to meet Fitzwilliam in Paris.

Before meeting the elder Kennedy, Fitzwilliam and Kathleen decided to spend two days in the resort of Cannes. They landed near Paris on a flight from London. They were preparing to take an eight-seat DeHavilland Dove airplane to Cannes. Because of a threat of violent thunderstorms, the pilot warned against the flight. But Fitzwilliam was intent on traveling to the coastal paradise and ordered the pilot to fly despite the warnings.

As predicted, the small plane ran directly into treacherous winds and unrelenting rain. Thrown off course, the plane tossed wildly before slamming into a mountain in the Rhône valley. All four aboard were killed.

Joe Kennedy, already in Europe, rushed to the scene of the accident and was called upon to identify his daughter's badly damaged body. She was buried in England, in the family plot of her husband.

Mother Rose refused to attend the funeral. The death hit Jack especially hard because of his close relationship with his younger sister.

The Marquess of Hartington married beautiful Kathleen Kennedy in 1944 (above). The marquess later died in action against the Germans in World War II. In 1948, Kathleen and her new fiancé, Lord Peter Fitzwilliam, were killed in a plane crash (opposite).

The death of Joe Junior in the war meant that Joe Kennedy's political ambitions for his oldest son were transferred to the younger Kennedy sons. Accordingly, each of them entered politics. Robert, Edward, and John are shown conferring (right) in a Senate committee meeting in 1959. Robert was counsel for the Senate rackets committee, and John was in his second Senate term. Young Teddy (below) became an Assistant District Attorney for Suffolk County, Massachusetts. Then–Secretary of State Kevin White, who eventually became the longtime mayor of Boston, administered the oath of office.

Ted's Expulsion from Harvard

The Kennedys have had a long association with Harvard University. That association was tarnished, however, by the youngest Kennedy son, Edward.

The future United States senator entered Harvard in 1950, following his father and his brothers. Bigger than his brothers had been, young Teddy made his mark on the football team. He had never been an outstanding student, and he was having difficulty with his Spanish. Another student agreed to take his Spanish exam for him.

Unfortunately for Teddy, the exam proctor recognized the subbing student and promptly informed the dean. The result: a one-year expulsion.

In time, Teddy was allowed to reenter the college, and eventually he graduated. The incident, however, would haunt him in his political career. While he was preparing to run for the Senate in 1962, a reporter from the *Boston Globe* planned to reveal it. After family negotiations with the reporter, which included intervention from President John Kennedy, a compromise was reached: The story appeared on page one, but below the fold, and was in the form of a confession under the headline "Ted Kennedy Tells About Harvard Examination Incident."

Years later, in 1980, while running for president, Teddy badly stumbled through a few words in Spanish to a group of Mexican Americans. "Well, what do you expect," one journalist was quoted as saying at the time. "It was the course he cheated on at Harvard."

Bobby Kennedy served as the special counsel to the Senate Subcommittee on Investigations (right), *working with Senators John McClellan, center, and Joseph McCarthy. Bobby reported to McCarthy's subcommittee* (below) *the shocking news that British-owned ships had been carrying Communist troops during the Korean War.*

Witch-hunt

In 1953, flamboyant Wisconsin Senator Joseph McCarthy began his sensational crusade against Communism and alleged Communists working within the United States government. Joe Kennedy was generally sympathetic to McCarthy's goals, and throughout his life, he arranged jobs for his children. He thought the anti-Communist crusade would provide a unique opportunity for his son Bobby to gain needed national exposure. He was right.

When McCarthy was appointed chairman of the Senate Subcommittee on Investigations, he hired Bobby as a legal counsel. Bobby made national press headlines when he testified before the committee that hundreds of Allied ships were delivering goods to Communist China. Then, after seven months of working for McCarthy, Bobby resigned.

The Kennedy family, particularly Joe, maintained allegiance to the Republican McCarthy.

The Army-McCarthy hearings (top) *were the media hit of 1954. Communist-baiter McCarthy, third from left, was advised by notorious lawyer Roy Cohn, fourth from left, who was under 30 at the time. Though Bobby Kennedy was now special counsel to the Senate committee conducting the investigation, the Kennedy family retained friendly ties to McCarthy. During the 1960s, Bobby engaged in a bitter battle with Teamsters president James Hoffa* (opposite), *here shown escorted by police on his way to address the 1958 meeting of the Western Conference of Teamsters. Kennedy's efforts to put Hoffa in jail finally succeeded in 1967. President Richard M. Nixon commuted Hoffa's sentence in 1971. On July 30, 1975, Hoffa disappeared from a Detroit restaurant and was never seen again.*

Less than a year later, Bobby was hired as the legal counsel for the Democratic minority on the committee investigating the charge McCarthy had acted improperly by arranging preferential treatment for a former employee who entered the Army as a private. Millions of Americans followed the Army-McCarthy hearings, as they were called, on television. Seeing McCarthy's steamroller tactics firsthand turned a large section of the public against him. His Communist witch-hunt, which ruined reputations without turning up hard evidence against anyone, was later widely denounced. Liberal Democrats loathed McCarthy.

Bobby was now working against his old boss, but he and McCarthy remained friendly. Many Democrats scorned the relationship, which was politically threatening not only for Bobby but also for his brother Jack. But the Kennedy family, particularly Joe, maintained allegiance to the Republican McCarthy. Joe contributed heavily to his campaigns. McCarthy was a frequent guest at the Kennedy homes in Palm Beach and Hyannis Port and even dated two of Bobby's sisters.

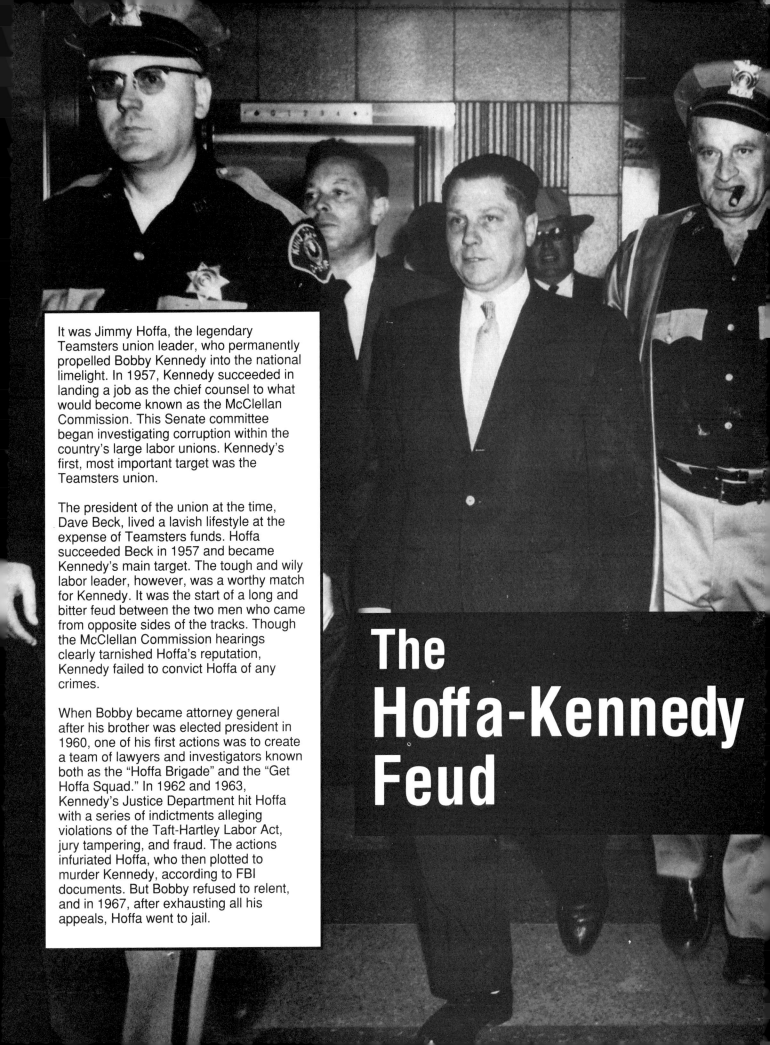

It was Jimmy Hoffa, the legendary Teamsters union leader, who permanently propelled Bobby Kennedy into the national limelight. In 1957, Kennedy succeeded in landing a job as the chief counsel to what would become known as the McClellan Commission. This Senate committee began investigating corruption within the country's large labor unions. Kennedy's first, most important target was the Teamsters union.

The president of the union at the time, Dave Beck, lived a lavish lifestyle at the expense of Teamsters funds. Hoffa succeeded Beck in 1957 and became Kennedy's main target. The tough and wily labor leader, however, was a worthy match for Kennedy. It was the start of a long and bitter feud between the two men who came from opposite sides of the tracks. Though the McClellan Commission hearings clearly tarnished Hoffa's reputation, Kennedy failed to convict Hoffa of any crimes.

When Bobby became attorney general after his brother was elected president in 1960, one of his first actions was to create a team of lawyers and investigators known both as the "Hoffa Brigade" and the "Get Hoffa Squad." In 1962 and 1963, Kennedy's Justice Department hit Hoffa with a series of indictments alleging violations of the Taft-Hartley Labor Act, jury tampering, and fraud. The actions infuriated Hoffa, who then plotted to murder Kennedy, according to FBI documents. But Bobby refused to relent, and in 1967, after exhausting all his appeals, Hoffa went to jail.

The Hoffa-Kennedy Feud

"CAMELOT"

A cold January day in 1961 saw the birth of the Kennedy presidency. The young president gave a memorable inaugural speech, seemingly heralding a bright future with a new generation in power. But Kennedy's term of office would be cut short.

The Romantic Myth

Beyond any international or national policy, the youthful Kennedy brought a new spirit to the White House. The New Generation, as it came to be known, was often highlighted in photographs of the president playing in the Oval Office with his young children. Kennedy and his attractive wife, Jackie, became the most celebrated couple in the world.

Camelot, the idealistic, romantic image of the Kennedy presidency, was a concept actually developed by Kennedy's widow, Jackie. After her husband's death, Jackie suggested the idea to pro-Kennedy journalist Theodore H. White. She proposed that Kennedy's 1,000 days in office were reminiscent of the halcyon glory of King Arthur's court. As a boy, she said, Jack often dreamed of performing valiant deeds like those of Ivanhoe or King Arthur's knights. Even before he was president, his favorite music before going to bed was from Lerner and Lowe's musical *Camelot*.

After Kennedy's death, the whole Kennedy family was idealized in numerous books. This showering of overwhelmingly positive biographies became known as the "Camelot School."

But everything was not rosy in the Kennedy White House.

The American public wanted to believe in the idyllic family life of the attractive first family. They loved to see photographs of the family together (above) *and of Caroline and John-John cavorting in the Oval Office* (below). *As Daddy went on with his business, John-John was photographed playing under the presidential desk* (opposite).

Mastering the Media

In 1960, John F. Kennedy beat his former friend and House colleague, Republican Richard M. Nixon, to become at age 43 the youngest man elected president of the United States. Jack had crisscrossed the country promising "to get the country moving again." His youthful energy and his charisma moved the crowds, and his agenda for "A New Generation" and "The New Frontier" was appealing. But the relatively new medium television is widely credited for propelling Kennedy to victory.

On September 25, 1960, Kennedy and Nixon participated in the first televised presidential debate, the first of a series of four. Most media commentators scored the debates a toss-up, and many radio listeners thought Nixon had the edge over Kennedy. But to the more than 85 million Americans who watched the event, Kennedy appeared as the cool, youthful, and charming debater. Vice President Nixon, sweating profusely through heavy makeup, did not appear to advantage under the piercing television lights. Many historians think the advantage Kennedy gained with the voters was enough to give him the election.

The 1960 presidential race gave birth to a common occurrence today: the televised debate (below). The debates with Nixon proved Kennedy to be a master of the television medium.

The relatively new medium television is widely credited for propelling Kennedy to victory.

Taken with Kennedy's appearance of youth and vigor, crowds greeted the charismatic candidate enthusiastically (above). But Kennedy had been hindered by health problems throughout his life. Kennedy easing his back pain in his rocking chair (above, right) became a familiar image. The public did not know he had Addison's disease.

Secret Health Problems

Far from being the hearty, vigorous young president of Camelot, John F. Kennedy suffered from a number of serious illnesses and almost constant back problems. A skinny child, Kennedy was born with an unstable back, a lifelong disability. At the age of two, Jack nearly died from a case of scarlet fever. In his childhood, he also suffered from measles, whooping cough, asthma, bronchitis, appendicitis, tonsillitis, influenza, allergies, and other ailments. His brother Bobby later remarked that Jack spent half his life in some kind of pain.

In 1935, halfway into his first term at Princeton, Jack again became ill and had to withdraw. He stayed in a Boston hospital for two months, suffering from "illness"—the exact illness was never disclosed. Afterward he switched to Harvard—his father's preferred school—and injured his back while playing football in his sophomore year. Rose Kennedy always attributed his back troubles to this injury.

Kennedy's back bothered him throughout his life. The press widely speculated that his back problems stemmed from the PT-109 incident during the war, thus giving his condition the aura of heroism, but problems with his back were a chronic, lifelong condition. He had to undergo several operations and at times could walk only with the aid of crutches.

Underlying all of Kennedy's physical complaints was his condition of Addison's disease, which was diagnosed in 1947. This is a serious condition in which the adrenal glands fail to produce enough hormones. Sufferers from Addison's disease become weak, lose weight, and can experience faintness. Joe Kennedy made sure that this condition was not made public for fear it would damage Jack's political career.

The Mafia Connection

In the 1960 election, Jack Kennedy received campaign contributions from an unusual source: the Mafia. It was an association that raises troubling questions about the former president's judgment and character.

By most accounts, it was singer Frank Sinatra who lined up mob support for the Kennedy bid. Joe Kennedy was also a conduit for the Mafia contributions. Many of the organized crime figures lining up to support Kennedy assumed their contributions would result in less scrutiny of their activities from the new administration.

But they didn't know that the new attorney general, Robert F. Kennedy, would launch a war against the Mafia, relentlessly pursuing criminal action against organized crime figures with a beefed-up staff of lawyers. The frustration of Chicago mob boss Sam Giancana was heard in an FBI wiretap of a conversation with a key lieutenant. "After all," Giancana said, "if I'm taking somebody's money, I'm gonna make sure this money is gonna do something, like, do you want it or don't you want it. If the money is accepted, maybe one of these days the guy will do me a favor." Another Mafia boss, Angelo Bruno of Philadelphia, tried to have Sinatra, through the Kennedys, block his deportation to Guatemala, but Bruno was unsuccessful.

JFK's Mistress—A Connection to the Mob

A second link connected JFK to the mob. In 1960, Frank Sinatra introduced Kennedy to Judith Campbell (later Exner), an attractive, 26-year-old woman. The two quickly began a two-year affair. Sinatra had also introduced the young woman to Mafia boss Sam Giancana, and Exner became a go-between from the president to the mob leader.

Since 1975, Exner has slowly revealed details about her relationship with Kennedy. In 1991, writer Anthony Summers reported that in an interview, Exner admitted she took large sums of money from Kennedy to Giancana several times during the 1960 election campaign. Exner also said that after Kennedy became president, she became a conduit between Kennedy and Giancana, several times carrying intelligence data to Giancana. She claims that Kennedy told her the data had to do with a plan to "eliminate" Cuban President Fidel Castro. Although the existence of such a plan has been known for years, Exner is the first to directly link JFK to it.

Apparently FBI director J. Edgar Hoover warned JFK that he knew all about this affair, and shortly afterward the relationship ended.

Though Kennedy was popular as a president, some of his associations and activities have cast a shadow on his judgment and character. Frank Sinatra (opposite, top) was friendly with Jack Kennedy. Many reports say he not only lined up Mafia support for Jack during his presidential campaign, he also lined up women for him. Judith Campbell Exner (above) claims that during her affair with Kennedy, she was his conduit to Chicago mobster Sam Giancana (opposite, bottom), carrying not only information but money between the two. When J. Edgar Hoover, the Machiavellian director of the FBI (left), let Kennedy know that he knew much about Kennedy's escapades, the affair with Exner ended.

Like Father, Like Son

His sexual prowess, like his father's, was one of the worst-kept secrets in Washington.

President Kennedy exchanged smiles with Angie Dickinson at his 1961 inaugural (below); she has always denied having an affair with him. Jayne Mansfield (opposite) was not impressed with Kennedy's lovemaking.

After his marriage to Jackie in 1953, Jack Kennedy often lived a dual life of devoted husband and playboy bachelor. His sexual prowess, like his father's, was one of the worst-kept secrets in Washington. While making the rounds of inaugural balls after his election to president, Jack took time to slip away from Jackie and attend a party given by Frank Sinatra. Actresses Angie Dickinson and Kim Novak, two women linked romantically to Kennedy, were there.

"Jack made no bones about the fact that he appreciated beautiful girls."

Kennedy's brother-in-law Peter Lawford introduced Kennedy to Dickinson and many of the other actresses he met and pursued. Dickinson campaigned for Kennedy and along with her husband, composer Burt Bacharach, became friendly with the Kennedy family. In 1975, Dickinson wrote an article denying any sexual relationship with Kennedy. "Jack Kennedy was the most exciting man in the world at the time I knew him," she wrote. "And to hear that I was having a romance with him is, of course, flattering. It was never rumored that he was in love with me, but Jack made no bones about the fact that he appreciated beautiful girls." Among the other beautiful women pursued by Jack were Jayne Mansfield and Gene Tierney, who was married to fashion designer Oleg Cassini.

Some of Kennedy's affairs might have been politically and diplomatically dangerous. JFK is reputed to have bedded Scandinavian beauty Inga Arvad, a friend of Adolph Hitler and a suspected Nazi spy during World War II. The affair was broken up by Jack's father. Brother Bobby ended another of Jack's relationships after he found out the woman, German-born Ellen Rometsch, was engaged in espionage for the Soviets.

Frank Sinatra and Kennedy's brother-in-law Peter Lawford (above) helped campaign for him and provided the Hollywood connection to many of the beautiful women Kennedy pursued. Sinatra was close enough to Jack to be seated next to him at a campaign fund-raiser (right).

Not All Women Succumbed

Kennedy's active libido is well documented, but his lovemaking did not always win praise. Jayne Mansfield complained to Lawford about Jack's coldness. "Jack's not much of a lover," Mansfield reportedly complained. "It's just in and out with him. No sweet talk before sex. . . . I feel sorry for his wife. . . ."

Some women actually said no to the appealing and powerful politician. Joan Fontaine, Shirley MacLaine, and Marlene Dietrich—who was reported to have carried on an affair with Jack's father, Joe—resisted his charms. As was his style, Jack had his eyes on actress Olivia de Havilland at a Hollywood party. Jack's friend Charles Spalding later recalled that they went to the actress's home for tea. "He leaned toward her and fixed her with a stare and he was working just as hard as he could, really boring in." According to Spalding, the actress was unimpressed. "Then, taking his leave, Jack, unable to take his eyes off Olivia, put his hand on the doorknob and walked straight into the hall closet!"

Some women were not overcome by the charms of Jack Kennedy. Actresses who said no to his advances included (top to bottom) *Joan Fontaine, Shirley MacLaine, and Olivia de Havilland.*

Marilyn Monroe

Like his father before him, John F. Kennedy romanced the reigning Hollywood sex goddess of his time.

JFK's object of desire was Marilyn Monroe, who was as much the symbol of glamour and sex appeal that Gloria Swanson had been in the '20s. Although neither Monroe nor Kennedy ever acknowledged a romantic relationship, a wealth of evidence suggests that the two carried on an affair.

They met at a dinner party arranged by Peter Lawford in 1954. The affair apparently first began several years later, when JFK arranged to spend several days with the screen star in Palm Springs. The relationship between the president and actress was reportedly so obvious by the 1960s that advisers cautioned the pair about its possible political ramifications.

Nonetheless, the affair continued after Jack's election to the presidency. According to C. David Heymann's book, *A Woman Named*

When Jack Kennedy met Marilyn Monroe, she was probably the most talked-about movie star in Hollywood. The embodiment of feminine beauty for millions, Marilyn felt proud to be having an affair with the president of the United States.

Marilyn was the ultimate in Hollywood glamour (above). **Her breathy singing of "Happy Birthday"** (opposite) **provided the finale at Kennedy's May 1962 Madison Square Garden birthday bash. That night was the last time she saw him. A few months later, she was dead.**

"It was only a lark for him, but she really fell for the guy, for what he represented."

Jackie, Monroe traveled aboard Air Force One disguised in a brown wig and sunglasses and met JFK for private liaisons at the Hotel Carlyle in New York.

"She was crazy about Jack," Lawford later said, according to Heymann. "She devised all sorts of madcap fantasies with herself in the starring role. She would have his children. She would take Jackie's place as first lady. It was only a lark for him, but she really fell for the guy, for what he represented."

Columnist Earl Wilson, who spent three years researching the relationship between Monroe and Kennedy, said Monroe was infatuated with the president and believed her "sexual pyrotechnics" with him eased his back pain. "Well, I think I made his back feel better," Wilson quoted Monroe as saying. He also quoted a source close to the actress as saying, "She was so proud to be the girl having an affair with the president of the United States, because that was important."

Their last rendezvous occurred at the Hotel Carlyle on May 19, 1962, two days before the president's 45th birthday. A massive birthday party and fund-raiser had been held in Madison Square Garden. A host of celebrities performed at the party, but Monroe provided the culmination. Dressed in a skin-colored, beaded gown so tight she literally had to be sewn into it, she had aroused the crowd with a sexy version of "Happy Birthday, Mr. President."

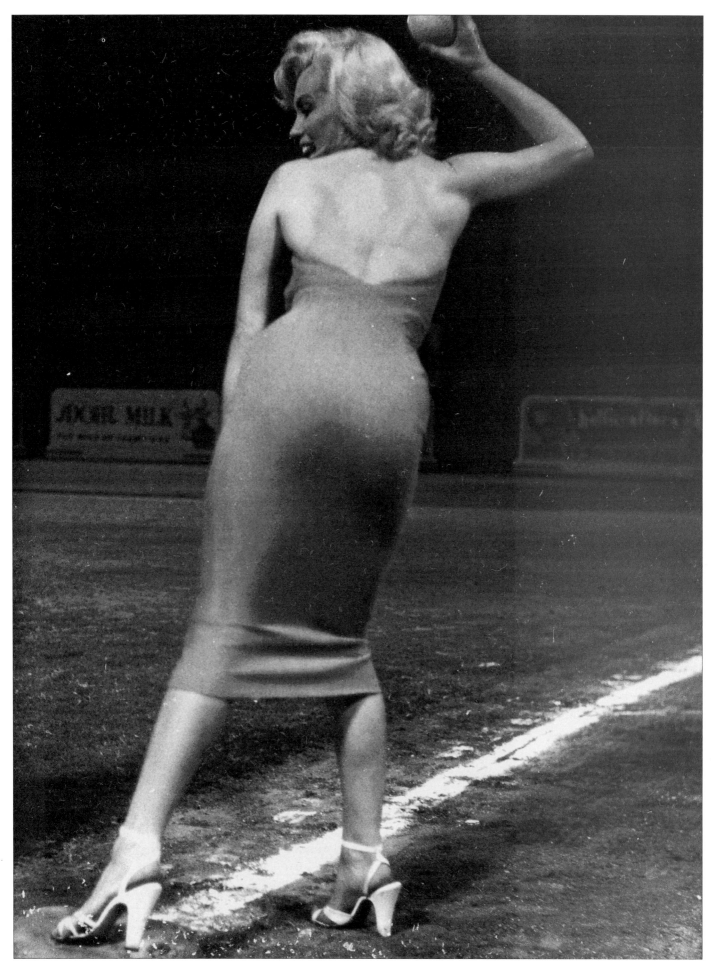

A host of persons, including Jimmy Hoffa and Sam Giancana, had an interest in gathering information detrimental to the president's reputation. The Kennedys became concerned that the Monroe affair was potentially dangerous. When Jack was tipped off that the Mafia knew about it, the president abruptly ended the affair. For Marilyn, it was a torturous finale. She phoned the White House often, hoping to talk to the president and rekindle his interest. Eventually she pulled a sure-fire weapon: She threatened to go to the press.

Jack sent Bobby to California to talk to Marilyn. Robert Kennedy, widely viewed as the most puritanical and faithful of the Kennedy clan, was soon having a serious extramarital affair with Marilyn Monroe—much more serious than Jack's. Apparently Marilyn hoped and believed Bobby would divorce his wife and marry her.

As is the case with John, no direct evidence links the two in a sexual relationship. A friend of Marilyn's, Jeanne Carmen, said she was at Monroe's apartment when Bobby Kennedy showed up one day. "I went to the door," she said. "I opened it up and there stands Bobby Kennedy. I went bo-ing! Marilyn came rushing out of the bathroom all of a sudden. She jumped into his arms, and they started kissing madly." Other witnesses said they saw Kennedy at her Brentwood home on a number of occasions in June and July of 1962. Kennedy's wife, Ethel, was fiercely loyal and devoted to her husband and dismissed any rumors about his infidelity.

But sometime during the summer of 1962, the Kennedys reportedly became aware of wiretaps on Monroe's telephone and Peter Lawford's. Monroe was told her connection with the Kennedys was over. She began to slide into depression and became more dependent on drugs and alcohol.

The Kennedys became concerned that the Monroe affair was potentially dangerous.

Jimmy Hoffa (top, left) *and Sam Giancana* (top, right), *no friends of the Kennedys, were eager for information about an affair between Jack and Marilyn Monroe* (opposite). *During the summer of 1962, Bobby Kennedy* (far right) *probably knew the telephones of Peter Lawford* (right) *and Monroe were being tapped.*

Mystery still clouds the apparent suicide of Marilyn Monroe; the details of her last night alive may never be known in full. The window of Marilyn Monroe's bedroom (right) may have been broken by her maid, who became alarmed after finding the actress dead. A hearse (below) carried the body of Hollywood's glamour queen away from her Brentwood home. On August 6 (opposite), her body was wheeled away from the Los Angeles County morgue to be taken to the Westwood Village Mortuary for funeral services.

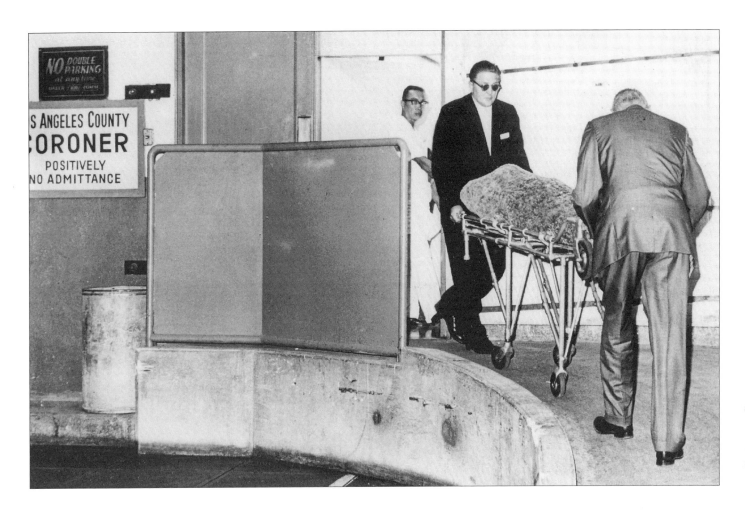

In the night of August 4–5, 1962, Monroe died of an overdose of barbiturates. The circumstances surrounding her death still remain controversial. Bobby Kennedy was in California on August 4, but where in California is much disputed. Kennedy claimed to have been in the San Francisco area, far from Hollywood, on that night. But many people have attested that he had appeared in Los Angeles that day.

Peter Lawford denied for years that Kennedy was in Los Angeles, but later he admitted Bobby went to Marilyn's house on August 4. Marilyn had been demanding that Bobby tell her to her face that the affair was over. The two reportedly had a stormy confrontation, with Bobby telling Monroe he could no longer see her.

Deeply depressed, Monroe took the drugs and apparently called Lawford. Someone called an ambulance. Later, Lawford may have entered her house and destroyed evidence connecting Marilyn to the Kennedys. Her death was ruled a suicide; several attempts to reopen the case over the years have failed.

In recent years, a New York man has stepped forward with the astonishing claim that he tape-recorded Bobby and Marilyn's last conversation as part of a surveillance effort. Wiretapper Bernard Spindel claims he bugged Marilyn's Brentwood home at the request of Jimmy Hoffa, who was looking for evidence to use against Bobby to counteract a grand jury probe being planned by the attorney general. Spindel claims the tapes were later stolen during an unauthorized 1967 raid on his home by the New York County District Attorney's office.

In the night of August 4–5, 1962, Monroe died of an overdose of barbiturates. The circumstances surrounding her death still remain controversial.

The Kennedy Presidency— Smashes and Fiascoes

The tone of the Kennedy presidency was set in one of the most memorable and best-known inauguration speeches in history, which most students regard as being principally the work of aide Ted Sorensen. "And so, my fellow Americans, ask not what your country can do for you; ask what you can do for your country. My fellow citizens of the world, ask not what America will do for you, but what together we can do for the freedom of man," the new president told the country on a cold January day.

Despite an impressive start, Kennedy stumbled early in his presidency with the embarrassing failure of the Bay of Pigs. The Bay of Pigs was a plan, born before Kennedy took office, to recruit a small army of Cuban exiles to invade Cuba and knock Communist Fidel Castro out of power. On April 17, 1961, a scaled-down version of the invasion was launched. It was a stunning defeat. Castro forces easily beat back the invaders within two days. Kennedy's reputation was damaged for supporting an invasion so poorly conceived and executed and for interfering in the affairs of a foreign country.

Ironically, it was events in Cuba more than a year later that dramatically boosted Kennedy's domestic and international power and prestige. It became apparent from U.S. military aerial photos that the Soviet Union had installed missile sites in Cuba capable of striking the United States. While Soviet ships were en route to Cuba carrying missiles for the sites, Kennedy made a dramatic announcement: The United States would blockade all Cuban ports. For four days, the world stood on edge, fearful of a war between the two superpowers. Finally, the Soviet ships turned back and the missile sites were dissembled.

Toppling Cuban leader Fidel Castro (top) was the object of the Bay of Pigs invasion in 1961; its failure was a low point in the Kennedy administration. In October 1962, Kennedy signed an order for the naval blockade of Cuba (right), which successfully forced the Soviet Union to withdraw missiles on the island.

The Soviets (opposite, top) assured JFK that the missile sites in Cuba were strictly defensive, but Kennedy knew they were more than that. Just a few days later, Kennedy announced the blockade.

Stoned in the White House?

Another of Jack's flings was the stunning, Vassar-educated Mary Pinchot Meyer. Meyer was the sister of Toni Bradlee, the wife of Ben Bradlee, who later became editor of the *Washington Post*. She secretly visited the White House at least 30 times. Ben Bradlee later admitted he read of the affair between the two in Meyer's personal diary, which was eventually destroyed by the CIA.

Reportedly, Meyer introduced Jack to marijuana and joked with him in the White House bedroom about being high when it came time to push the nuclear war button. Meyer was murdered in 1964. She was shot twice in the head while taking her normal morning walk.

DALLAS
NOVEMBER 22, 1963

The Shot That Ended an Era

President and Mrs. Kennedy waved and smiled at the friendly Dallas crowd (previous pages). Just minutes later, shots rang out and the president was hit by the bullets of an assassin. A Secret Service man and Mrs. Kennedy leaned over the slumping body of the president. The limousine immediately sped toward the closest hospital (inset).

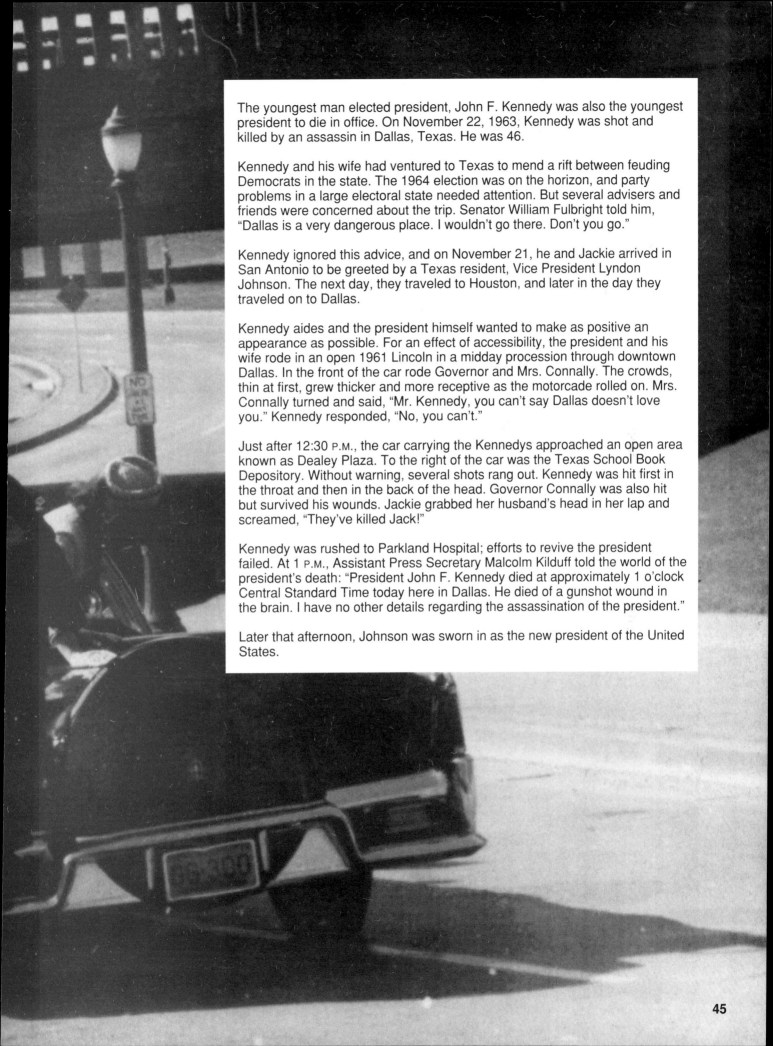

The youngest man elected president, John F. Kennedy was also the youngest president to die in office. On November 22, 1963, Kennedy was shot and killed by an assassin in Dallas, Texas. He was 46.

Kennedy and his wife had ventured to Texas to mend a rift between feuding Democrats in the state. The 1964 election was on the horizon, and party problems in a large electoral state needed attention. But several advisers and friends were concerned about the trip. Senator William Fulbright told him, "Dallas is a very dangerous place. I wouldn't go there. Don't you go."

Kennedy ignored this advice, and on November 21, he and Jackie arrived in San Antonio to be greeted by a Texas resident, Vice President Lyndon Johnson. The next day, they traveled to Houston, and later in the day they traveled on to Dallas.

Kennedy aides and the president himself wanted to make as positive an appearance as possible. For an effect of accessibility, the president and his wife rode in an open 1961 Lincoln in a midday procession through downtown Dallas. In the front of the car rode Governor and Mrs. Connally. The crowds, thin at first, grew thicker and more receptive as the motorcade rolled on. Mrs. Connally turned and said, "Mr. Kennedy, you can't say Dallas doesn't love you." Kennedy responded, "No, you can't."

Just after 12:30 P.M., the car carrying the Kennedys approached an open area known as Dealey Plaza. To the right of the car was the Texas School Book Depository. Without warning, several shots rang out. Kennedy was hit first in the throat and then in the back of the head. Governor Connally was also hit but survived his wounds. Jackie grabbed her husband's head in her lap and screamed, "They've killed Jack!"

Kennedy was rushed to Parkland Hospital; efforts to revive the president failed. At 1 P.M., Assistant Press Secretary Malcolm Kilduff told the world of the president's death: "President John F. Kennedy died at approximately 1 o'clock Central Standard Time today here in Dallas. He died of a gunshot wound in the brain. I have no other details regarding the assassination of the president."

Later that afternoon, Johnson was sworn in as the new president of the United States.

The Accused Assassin

Lee Harvey Oswald, the man accused of assassinating President Kennedy, was born in New Orleans in 1939. His father having died before his birth, he lacked a strong father figure during most of his childhood. While growing up, he was often characterized as a loner and an occasional troublemaker. His youth was without any significant achievement.

Oswald's adult life, however, was an interesting combination of foreign adventure and hardened leftist beliefs. After a three-year stint in the military, Oswald defected to the Soviet Union, where he met his wife, Marina. They had two daughters. In 1962, with the assistance of a U.S. repatriation loan, Oswald and his new family returned to the United States.

By all accounts, Oswald led a bizarre life upon his return to his native country. Friends suspected he was beating his wife, and she in turn criticized her husband's sexual inadequacy. For a brief period of time, the couple separated. Oswald became entranced by leftist literature, frequently reading *Worker* and *Militant.* In New Orleans, Oswald became part of a local pro-Cuba movement and became a staunch supporter of Fidel Castro. He was arrested for trying to distribute pro-Castro pamphlets. And two months before the assassination, he went to Mexico City and visited the Cuban and Russian embassies there.

During the early 1960s, Oswald took an interest in the Kennedy family and the Bouviers, the family of Kennedy's wife. He checked out books on the president, and a Russian immigrant with ties to the Bouvier family filled Oswald with tales regarding the family.

Lee Harvey Oswald is holding his mail-order rifle that he later used to shoot Kennedy (opposite) *in this snapshot taken by his wife, Marina. In his other hand he holds a Communist newspaper. The 24-year-old Oswald* (top) *was taken into custody after the shooting. Oswald took aim at the president from a room on the sixth floor of the Texas School Book Depository* (bottom)*. The arrow points to the location from which Oswald fired the fatal shots.*

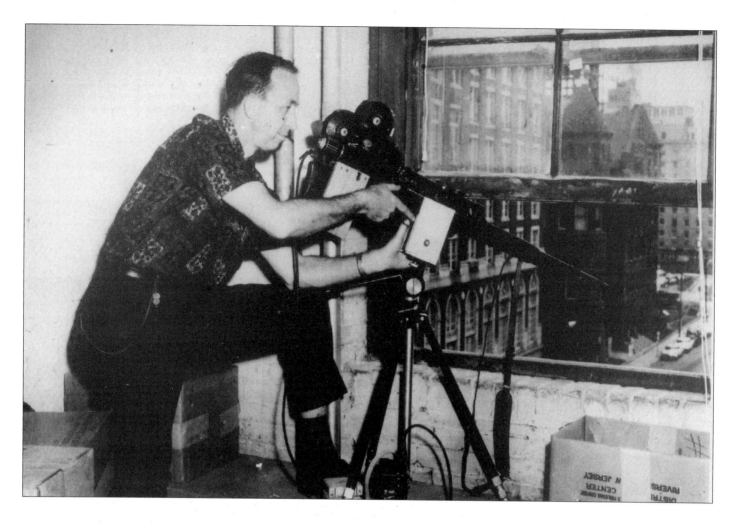

Shortly after 12:30 P.M., Oswald took aim from a window on the sixth floor of the building and fired the shots that would change the world.

In 1964, an FBI agent reenacted the actions of Oswald from the sixth floor of the Texas School Book Depository (above). The agent, working for the Warren Commission, used a 6.5mm Mannlicher-Carcano rifle found in the room after the shooting. A camera mounted on the weapon during the reenactment recorded the scene on the street below through the rifle's telescopic scope.

Ruth Paine, a friend of Oswald's wife, helped the soon-to-be assassin land a job at the Texas School Book Depository on October 15, just over a month before the president's visit to Dallas. On November 19, three days before the presidential visit, the motorcade route was announced. Kennedy would pass directly in front of the depository. On the day of JFK's visit, Oswald arrived at the book depository at 8 A.M. He carried the murder weapon, a mail-order, high-powered rifle, in a brown bag. Shortly after 12:30 P.M., Oswald took aim from a window on the sixth floor of the building and fired the shots that would change the world.

Oswald fled the scene, went home, stayed briefly and left. At some point after leaving his rooming house, Oswald shot and killed Dallas police officer J. D. Tippet. The circumstances of that shooting are sketchy. Oswald was arrested a short time later for the killings of Tippet and the president. The next day, November 23, Oswald was arraigned for both killings. As police tried to move him to a new jail, Dallas nightclub owner Jack Ruby shot and killed Oswald.

In front of stunned police officers, Ruby flashed a Colt .38 and shot Oswald.

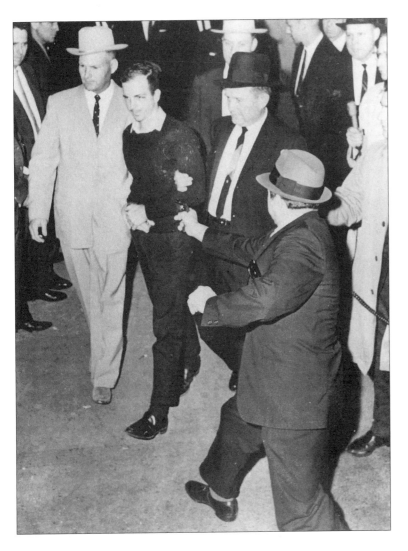

A photographer captured the dramatic moment (left) when nightclub owner Jack Ruby stepped forward and shot Lee Harvey Oswald as he was being transfered to another jail. Ruby delivered a fatal shot into Oswald's stomach. The Dallas nightclub owner (below) *died before serving any jail time for Oswald's murder.*

Jack Ruby

Shortly after being arraigned for the murder of President Kennedy, Dallas police were attempting to transfer Lee Harvey Oswald from the city jail to the county jail. A large crowd of onlookers had buzzed around the courthouse and jail the day after the assassination. Mingling in the crowd was Dallas nightclub owner Jack Ruby. In front of stunned police officers, Ruby flashed a Colt .38 and shot Oswald. In the aftermath of the shooting, Ruby claimed that he had been angered by the shooting of the president and wanted to protect Kennedy's widow from the pain she would experience attending Oswald's trial.

In some conspiracy theories, Ruby was sent by mob leaders to stifle Oswald. While evidence linking Ruby to some of these persons is compelling, there are no solid links to a conspiracy. He died in 1967 while awaiting a retrial on the charge he murdered Oswald.

The Zapruder Film

A stunned Mrs. Kennedy turned toward her wounded husband (opposite, top) only an instant after he was struck by bullets. Jackie's horror is clear on her face (opposite, bottom) as she realized her husband had been shot. Mrs. Kennedy crawled for help (above) as Secret Service agents rushed to the president's car.

A home movie camera captured the assassination of President Kennedy in horrifying detail. Businessman Abraham Zapruder, on a visit to Dallas, decided to watch the presidential motorcade on November 22, 1963. When he first set out, he forgot his camera, an eight-millimeter Bell & Howell movie camera, but he turned around to fetch it. He set up near the Texas School Book Depository. Zapruder focused on the motorcade as it came toward him and photographed the president as he was pelted by the assassin's bullets.

The 18-second film has been cut, spliced, and examined frame by frame by investigators probing the assassination. It is one of the few absolutely solid pieces of evidence in the murder of Kennedy. Zapruder sold his film to *Life* magazine for $150,000, and the magazine published frame-by-frame photos. It wasn't until March 1975, however, that the moving film was shown on television. To this day, the Zapruder family charges a $30,000 fee for the commercial use of the film.

A home movie camera captured the assassination of President Kennedy in horrifying detail.

Was It a Conspiracy?

In a 1978 experiment (above), *a Dallas police sharpshooter fired a rifle from behind a fence in Dealey Plaza while acoustics experts recorded the sound. The exercise was part of an effort to determine whether a fourth shot was fired from a location other than the Texas School Book Depository. Some conspiracy theorists believe Teamsters president Jimmy Hoffa* (opposite, top) *may have been behind the killing of Kennedy as retaliation for Bobby Kennedy's crackdown on union fraud. Cuban President Fidel Castro* (opposite, bottom) *is also mentioned as a possible source for Oswald's act.*

A popular subject for debate among historians and politics buffs is the motivation for the assassination of John F. Kennedy. The killing of Oswald buried many of the answers. As a result, an array of so-called conspiracy theories regarding the assassination continue to swirl to this day. Each theory has a school of supporters who point to pieces of physical evidence to support their cause. In reality, the full set of circumstances surrounding the assassination may never be known. Here, however, are some of the theories:

● The mob, still angry over its perception that JFK double-crossed it after helping him in the 1960 election, arranged for the assassination. A Philadelphia gangster was recorded in a conversation with an associate suggesting the murder of the president might be a good idea. The Kennedy administration was making a crackdown on organized crime a top priority.

● A related theory holds that New Orleans mob boss Carlos Marcello organized the shooting to thwart Bobby Kennedy's attempts to have him deported. Oswald was born in New Orleans and was living in the city before moving to Texas weeks before the assassination. In addition, Marcello had strong ties to the Texas organized crime families.

• The Teamsters union was behind the assassination. Teamsters president Jimmy Hoffa had a long and bitter feud with Attorney General Robert Kennedy. The Teamsters, who believed Bobby was involved in a ruthless personal vendetta against the union, may have acted to thwart his power by killing the president, according to supporters of this theory.

• Cuban President Fidel Castro orchestrated the assassination after becoming infuriated by CIA plans to have him killed. Oswald was arrested for distributing pro-Castro leaflets only months before the assassination. He had also lived in Russia and visited the Cuban embassy in Mexico City.

Despite the popular notion of a conspiracy to kill President Kennedy, two official federal investigations into the assassination failed to conclude the killing was a conspiracy. President Lyndon Johnson, himself the target of some conspiracy theorists, decided to create a commission to investigate the murder. The Warren Commission, named after chairman and Supreme Court Chief Justice Earl Warren, concluded in 1964 that Oswald acted alone. It did not totally discount the existence of a conspiracy, but concluded there was no evidence to support any conspiracy.

The Warren Commission never heard any evidence regarding attempts by the Kennedy administration to murder Castro. In fact, years later it was apparent the FBI, CIA, and other agencies and persons had withheld information from the commission.

In 1978, the House Select Committee on Assassinations reached no final conclusion on the Kennedy case. Although the committee did give strong support to the theory New Orleans mob boss Marcello might have been behind the assassination, it did not endorse the theory. It did, however, accept the testimony of an acoustical expert who said the shots were fired from two locations along the motorcade route. The committee also said Kennedy "was probably assassinated as a result of a conspiracy."

An array of so-called conspiracy theories regarding the assassination continue to swirl to this day.

Funeral for a President

The flag-draped casket of the assassinated president lay in state in the Capitol rotunda. Mrs. Kennedy was flanked by her brothers-in-law Attorney General Robert Kennedy and Senator Edward Kennedy on her final visit.

The funeral for slain president John F. Kennedy brought together an unequaled array of world leaders and dignitaries. It was truly a global event—through the new technology of satellites, it was captured by television and broadcast worldwide.

After the assassination, Kennedy's body was flown to Washington. In the Capitol rotunda, hundreds of thousands of mourners paid their silent respects to the president on the eve of his funeral. A long funeral procession marched from the White House to St. Matthew's Cathedral. After a funeral mass, the casket was brought from the church. Outside, three-year-old John F. Kennedy, Jr., brought tears to the eyes of the world with a salute to his slain father. Again, the funeral procession formed and wound through the Capitol trailed by Black Jack, the riderless horse.

Kennedy was buried at Arlington National Cemetery. Fifty jets, representing the fifty states, screeched across the sky accompanied by Air Force One. A bugler played taps and a military guard presented a 21-gun salute.

Mrs. Kennedy was escorted by the president's brother Bobby throughout the period after her husband died. It was Bobby who helped his sister-in-law light the Eternal Flame.

The young widow and her children (opposite) *stood outside St. Matthew's Cathedral in Washington. The president's son saluted the casket of his father. It was John-John's third birthday. The tradition of the riderless horse* (above), *boots turned backward in the stirrups, originated with President Lincoln's funeral. Heads of state and other leaders throughout the world* (below) *journeyed to Washington for Kennedy's funeral.*

THE THIRD BROTHER FALLS

The celebration was over, and the ballroom of the Ambassador Hotel in Los Angeles was littered with debris. Earlier, 2,000 supporters had cheered Senator Robert Kennedy's victory in the California presidential primary. But as he was leaving the ballroom, he was felled by an assassin's bullet.

48 Hours in Los Angeles

A smiling Robert Kennedy, accompanied by his wife, Ethel, and campaign aides, talked with journalists and supporters about his primary win. Moments later, as he was leaving to attend a press conference in a nearby room, Kennedy and five others were shot. Still conscious (inset), Kennedy lay gravely wounded on the floor of the hotel's pantry.

Ever since JFK's assassination in Dallas in 1963, friends and family members feared Bobby would become the next target of a madman's bullet. Those fears became reality on June 5, 1968.

Three days earlier, a group of youths had set off a string of firecrackers while Bobby's motorcade drove through the streets of Los Angeles. Bobby's wife, Ethel, perhaps reminded of the president's assassination, shielded herself by crouching in a corner of the car as the fireworks exploded behind her. Bobby, riding with her, didn't move. It was, to some, a dress rehearsal of what would happen later.

On June 4, the day of the California primary, Bobby, surrounded by his wife and several of his children, watched the returns on television in his suite at the Los Angeles Ambassador Hotel. The room had taken on a festive atmosphere. Astronaut John Glenn was there, as was columnist Jimmy Breslin and a host of other Kennedy supporters.

Shortly after the polls closed, CBS projected a Kennedy victory, and by 10 P.M. it was apparent that Bobby was indeed the winner. Bobby did interviews with the television networks; then, shortly before midnight, he left the suite for the Ambassador's ballroom, where some 2,000 happy supporters awaited him. With Ethel at his side, Bobby thanked the cheering crowd. Then he left the podium to attend a prearranged press conference in the nearby Colonial Room. To get to the press conference, he walked through a pantry adjacent to the hotel's main ballroom.

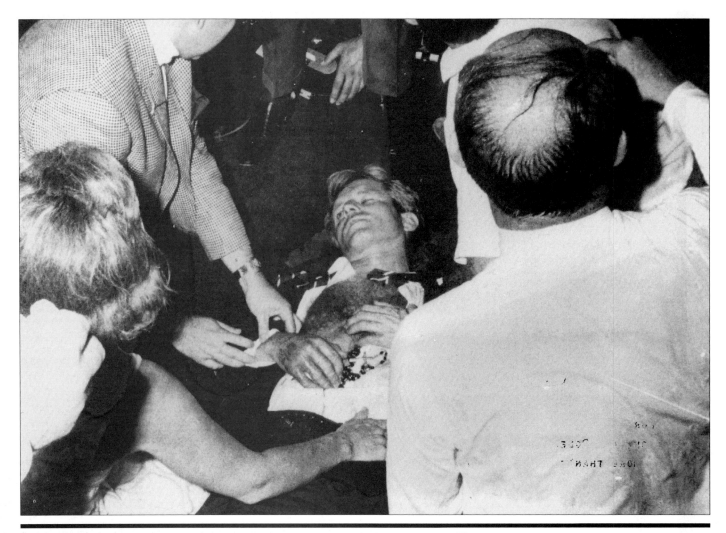

The Death of the Candidate

Suddenly the noisy celebration in the ballroom was pierced by the sound of gunfire. At least 13 shots were fired. Three of them tore through Bobby's body; others struck five bystanders.

Ex–football player Rosie Grier, Bobby's bodyguard, helped to wrestle the gunman to the ground. He was later identified as an Arab, 24-year-old Sirhan Sirhan. On the floor, Bobby lay bleeding from wounds to his head and neck. By the time Ethel saw her husband, someone had placed a rosary in his hand. Ethel cradled Bobby's head in her lap, talking to him softly as his life slowly ebbed away.

At Central Receiving Hospital, doctors worked frantically to save the dying candidate's life. "I could see that he was like a blob of Jell-O that you took out of the refrigerator. I immediately realized that he was probably gone, but of course I couldn't be sure of it," Dr. Victor F. Bazilauskas would later recall in Lester David's book *Ethel: The Story of Mrs. Robert F. Kennedy*. Bobby showed no signs of life. Then Dr. Bazilauskas injected him with adrenalin and Bobby's heart again started pumping.

Because his head wound required immediate surgery, Bobby was moved to another hospital three blocks away. About 25 hours after a team of surgeons performed the delicate brain operation, Bobby died. Ethel, Jackie, Ted, Pat Lawford, and Jean and Stephen Smith were by his side.

By the time Ethel saw her husband, someone had placed a rosary in his hand.

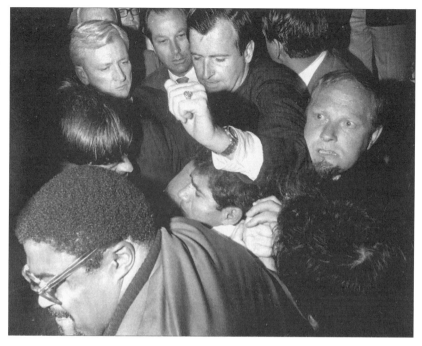

Clutching a rosary placed in his hand by a hotel kitchen worker (opposite), *the mortally wounded senator was comforted by aides and his wife, Ethel. Meanwhile, in another part of the pantry (left), Sirhan Sirhan, in the center of the photo, was being restrained by Kennedy aides including Rosie Grier, in the foreground, the senator's bodyguard who was a former Los Angeles Rams tackle. The funeral for the slain senator (below) was held in St. Patrick's Cathedral in New York. Senator Edward Kennedy, the last remaining Kennedy son, delivered the eulogy.*

CALIF PRISON
B 21014
B S SIRHAN
5 23 69

Conspiracy Theories Abound

Bobby's death fueled even more theories of conspiracy than his brother Jack's did. Among the more popular theories, and the one admitted to by Sirhan, is that the Arab assassin gunned down RFK because of the candidate's support for Israel.

Author Truman Capote, a friend of Jacqueline Kennedy, promoted his own theory that Sirhan and a handful of accomplices may have actually been highly trained Arab triggermen bent on assassinating all U.S. political leaders in a bid to bring the United States to its knees.

Other conspiracy theorists claim Teamsters boss Jimmy Hoffa used his connections with the Mafia to have RFK killed in retaliation for his tenacious investigation into Hoffa and the mob during his days as attorney general.

One of the more interesting theories comes from former CIA operative Robert Morrow. In his book *The Senator Must Die: The Murder of Robert F. Kennedy,* Morrow claims Bobby was killed by members of the Iranian secret police. The motive was to prevent him from becoming president, when he could cut off American support to the Shah of Iran.

Morrow argues that Sirhan acted as a diversion while the real assassin shot Bobby at point-blank range with a camera gun from behind. The second-gunman theory is in fact supported by ballistics tests, which concluded that the fatal shot to Bobby's head was not fired from Sirhan's gun. Witnesses to the shooting also report that Sirhan fired at RFK from the front. The autopsy, however, shows that all shots struck him from behind.

Fueling the second-gunman theory are FBI photographs of the shooting scene, which show that at least 13 bullets were fired. Given the fact that Sirhan's .22-caliber handgun held only eight rounds, it is likely the remaining bullets came from another weapon.

In his book *Contract on America: The Mafia Murder of President John F. Kennedy,* author David E. Scheim claims the second gunman was actually a hotel security guard who stood behind Bobby and pulled his gun at the first burst of bullets. The security guard's gun, claims Scheim, was "the only gun in the exact position to inflict Kennedy's wounds." Sirhan, incarcerated in prison in California, has continually maintained that he acted alone to kill RFK.

An enduring mystery is the woman in the polka-dot dress. Numerous witnesses claim to have seen a man along with a woman in a polka-dot dress with Sirhan prior to the shooting. The couple was also seen later, fleeing the pantry after RFK had been gunned down. Despite relentless efforts to track down the now-famous woman in the polka-dot dress, investigators have never been able to find her or her companion.

Sirhan Bishara Sirhan (opposite) *pleaded guilty to killing Senator Kennedy, allegedly in retaliation for Kennedy's support for Israel. The police mug shot* (opposite, inset) *was taken nearly a year later; the date is under his name. Though many people were present at the shooting and assisted in restraining Sirhan* (left), *RFK's assassination has sparked a number of conspiracy theories.*

Another Plane Crash

Less than a year after the assassination of Jack, tragedy once again nearly struck the Kennedy family. In 1964, a chartered plane carrying Ted, the pilot, and three others crashed in dense fog just outside Springfield, Massachusetts.

The news of the crash sent a jolt through the Kennedy clan. Kathleen had died in a plane crash in France, and Joe Junior had been killed during World War II when the military plane he was piloting exploded.

Ted Kennedy had been elected to fill his brother Jack's senate seat in 1962. On June 19, 1964, Teddy, his aide Edward Moss, and Senator and Mrs. Birch Bayh were en route to the Massachusetts Democratic State Convention, where Kennedy was to receive the party endorsement for a full term. Bayh was to be the keynote speaker. A key Senate vote for a civil rights bill had delayed the party in Washington, and they set out on a chartered six-seat Aero Commander. The party enjoyed a trouble-free flight until the weather began to sour around New York City. Thunderstorms began to rock the plane, and dense fog promised a complicated landing.

An experienced pilot was at the controls, and Kennedy himself had piloted a small plane in the western Massachusetts area before. As the plane began to descend, it became apparent the dense fog and low visibility would require an instrument landing. As the plane lowered toward the runway, the belly of the aircraft struck the tops of trees. The plane broke apart and crashed in nearby farmland.

The Bayhs escaped relatively unharmed. The pilot was killed. And Moss died from injuries suffered in the crash. Kennedy was rushed to a hospital in nearby Northampton with critical injuries. The young senator suffered three crushed vertebrae, two cracked ribs, and a punctured lung. He spent six months recovering, but he was able to walk into the Senate without any assistance when he returned to Washington.

President Lyndon Johnson talked with Kennedy and his wife, Joan in the hospital (opposite). The Stryker frame in the background was used to help speed his recovery from back injuries.

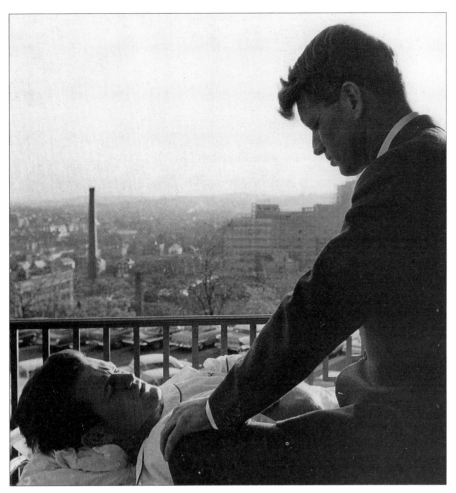

As the plane lowered toward the runway, the belly of the aircraft struck the tops of trees. The plane broke apart and crashed in nearby farmland.

The twisted wreckage of the small plane (opposite) that was taking Teddy Kennedy to the Massachusetts Democratic State Convention lay crumpled in a field near Springfield, Massachusetts. Kennedy escaped the June 19, 1964, crash with serious injuries. He was still recovering in November (left), when he and his brother, Bobby, talked at a Boston hospital.

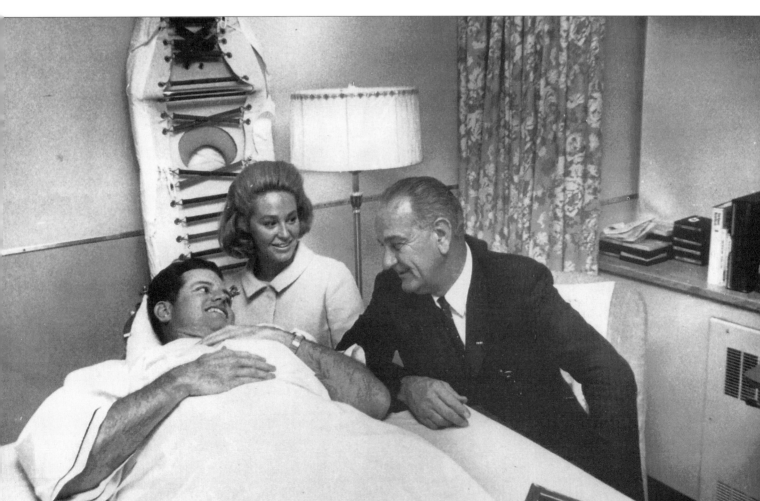

A Party on Chappaquiddick

A car approaches Dike Bridge, which crosses Poucha Pond, a small tidal pool on the island of Chappaquiddick.

Authorities conferred near Kennedy's black Oldsmobile shortly after it was pulled from Poucha Pond. The body of Mary Jo Kopechne, the only passenger, had already been removed from inside. The inset photo shows Kopechne at the time of her graduation from Caldwell College for Women around 1962.

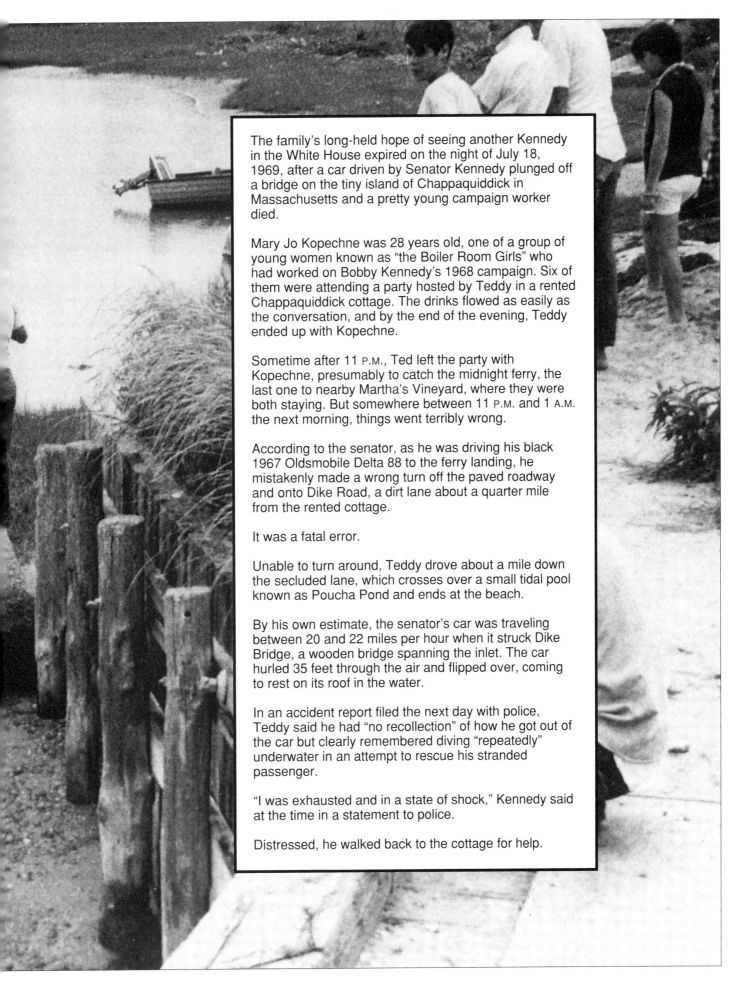

The family's long-held hope of seeing another Kennedy in the White House expired on the night of July 18, 1969, after a car driven by Senator Kennedy plunged off a bridge on the tiny island of Chappaquiddick in Massachusetts and a pretty young campaign worker died.

Mary Jo Kopechne was 28 years old, one of a group of young women known as "the Boiler Room Girls" who had worked on Bobby Kennedy's 1968 campaign. Six of them were attending a party hosted by Teddy in a rented Chappaquiddick cottage. The drinks flowed as easily as the conversation, and by the end of the evening, Teddy ended up with Kopechne.

Sometime after 11 P.M., Ted left the party with Kopechne, presumably to catch the midnight ferry, the last one to nearby Martha's Vineyard, where they were both staying. But somewhere between 11 P.M. and 1 A.M. the next morning, things went terribly wrong.

According to the senator, as he was driving his black 1967 Oldsmobile Delta 88 to the ferry landing, he mistakenly made a wrong turn off the paved roadway and onto Dike Road, a dirt lane about a quarter mile from the rented cottage.

It was a fatal error.

Unable to turn around, Teddy drove about a mile down the secluded lane, which crosses over a small tidal pool known as Poucha Pond and ends at the beach.

By his own estimate, the senator's car was traveling between 20 and 22 miles per hour when it struck Dike Bridge, a wooden bridge spanning the inlet. The car hurled 35 feet through the air and flipped over, coming to rest on its roof in the water.

In an accident report filed the next day with police, Teddy said he had "no recollection" of how he got out of the car but clearly remembered diving "repeatedly" underwater in an attempt to rescue his stranded passenger.

"I was exhausted and in a state of shock," Kennedy said at the time in a statement to police.

Distressed, he walked back to the cottage for help.

The Morning After

The next morning, a casually dressed Teddy, appearing refreshed despite having swum across the small channel from Chappaquiddick to Martha's Vineyard the night before, stood on the porch of the Shiretown Inn in Edgartown, where he was staying for the weekend. There, he calmly discussed with several hotel guests a sailboat race that had occurred the day before.

Witnesses would later say he gave no impression that something was horribly wrong.

But then his cousin Joe Gargan and another friend, Paul Markham, both of whom had been at the party, showed up. They were distressed that Kennedy had not yet reported the accident, which had occurred some eight hours earlier. The car had by now been discovered by a man and a boy who were fishing near the bridge. It wouldn't be long before Kopechne's body would be found.

Curious spectators lined Dike Bridge (top) as investigators inspected the damage to Kennedy's car, which had just been towed from the swirling currents. Diver John Farrar (above) checked the car's interior where Kopechne's body was found. The car (opposite, bottom) sustained damage to the passenger-side doors as well as the hood.

When diver John Farrar went underwater to inspect the overturned Olds, he knew immediately that Kopechne didn't drown.

Her body, Farrar would later say, was in "a conscious position" with her hands gripping the edge of the back seat and her head at the floorboards where the last bit of air would likely have been.

Farrar removed her body and then watched as a medical examiner pushed on her chest, sending a tiny bit of water trickling out of her mouth.

"The water in the lungs of a drowning victim is usually measured in quarts. Hers was about half a teacup," the diver would later say. "She never drowned. She suffocated—and after a considerable amount of time."

About the same time Kopechne's body—dressed in slacks, a blouse and lacy blue brassiere but without underpants—was being pulled from eight feet of water, Teddy was at the Edgartown police station filing a report on the accident.

The report, which later sold for $40,000, contained just 15 short sentences by the senator describing the accident.

The first picture of Kennedy taken that morning (left) shows him rushing from the Chappaquiddick ferry on his way to report the accident.

The Cover-up

By most accounts, Teddy's decision to cover up his role in the accident began almost immediately after his car plunged into Poucha Pond.

Leo Damore's best-selling book *Senatorial Privilege: The Chappaquiddick Cover-Up* describes how Paul Markham and Joe Gargan dove for Kopechne, but the current was too strong. Gargan's recollection is that after discussing the options with Kennedy, the three reached no conclusion. The senator said he would "take care" of it and dove fully dressed into the water to swim back to his hotel. Gargan assumed Kennedy meant he would report the incident; Kennedy apparently assumed his friends would handle the matter.

He had hoped it would look as though Kopechne, driving alone on the unfamiliar island, plunged over the unrailed bridge on her own, according to Damore.

Concerned for his future political career, Teddy soon spawned a series of actions that colored the investigation into Kopechne's death right from the start.

But Gargan and Markham balked. And so, nearly 10 hours after Kopechne met her death, Teddy claimed responsibility for the accident.

Had the matter ended there, few, perhaps, would have known.

But, concerned for his future political career, Teddy soon spawned a series of actions that colored the investigation into Kopechne's death right from the start.

Within hours of the time her body was discovered, the five remaining "Boiler Room Girls" were whisked from the island before they could be interviewed by police. In fact everyone at the party on the night of July 18, including the senator, suddenly became unavailable for police interviews.

The investigation turned into a political hot potato.

District Attorney Edmund S. Dinis, well aware of the powerful political pull the Kennedys exerted, initially balked at taking the investigation beyond the routine stage. Soon, however, the clamor from the press was so overwhelming that, 12 days after Kopechne's death, Dinis was forced to ask the court to hold an inquest into the accident.

Reporters tackled Kennedy (opposite), wearing an orthopedic collar, as he and his wife, Joan, returned to Hyannis Port from Kopechne's funeral in Pennsylvania. Six months later, authorities held an inquest into the car accident that killed Kopechne. Among those questioned were Paul F. Markham (top), a former U.S. Attorney and friend of the senator, and Joseph Gargan (left), Kennedy's cousin, both shown here outside the Dukes County Courthouse on Martha's Vineyard, where the inquest was held. Both men had attended the party on Chappaquiddick the night the senator's car plunged off Dike Bridge. They were the two friends Kennedy consulted just after the accident.

Teddy Resorts to a Nationally Televised Plea

The media's clamor for more information was also wearing on the senator. Three days after Kopechne was buried in a tiny cemetery in Plymouth, Pennsylvania, and the same day he received a two-month suspended sentence and a year's probation for leaving the scene of an accident, Teddy gave a nationally televised speech.

A somber Teddy explained his version of events, denying any relationship with Kopechne and saying he was not drunk when the accident occurred. Then, in a stunning admission marked with a reference to his brother John, he told viewers he was contemplating resigning from the Senate after seven years in office.

Within minutes, hundreds of callers began phoning Teddy's Boston office with supportive messages for the senator. Telegrams from across the nation flooded in. The voters, so drawn to his brothers Jack and Bobby, had thrown their support behind him. The scandal surrounding the accident would not mar his political standing.

The Inquest

The threat of an inquest was troubling to the Kennedy family, but Teddy, unbeknownst to many, had an ace in the hole. His name was Bernie Flynn. Flynn was an investigator for the Dukes County District Attorney's office and a Kennedy sympathizer.

"I never believed Kennedy was driving that car," Flynn would say years later. "I thought he was covering up for someone else."

Concerned for the senator's political future and eager to help him out, Flynn soon contacted Teddy's brother-in-law Stephen Smith and arranged two meetings.

Smith, known as the Kennedys' "fixer" for his ability to get family members out of tight jams, and Kennedy lawyer Herbert "Jack" Miller met Flynn at airports in Washington and Boston, where the investigator outlined the state's case against the senator.

According to Flynn's account, prosecutors had three witnesses who could possibly jeopardize Teddy's case.

One was Christopher "Huck" Look, a deputy sheriff who saw a car similar to Teddy's black Olds driving on Chappaquiddick about an hour after the senator claimed the accident occurred. The other two were guests of the Shiretown Inn, who would testify that Teddy did not

After Kennedy's extraordinary national statement, his constituents rallied behind him. Two months to the day after the accident, Kennedy began making public addresses again (opposite). The Boiler Room Girls (above) returned to Martha's Vineyard for the inquest. The women, who were Rosemary Keough on the left, Mary Ellen Lyons, her sister Nance Lyons, Susan Tannenbaum, and Esther Newberg on the right, testified in support of Kennedy.

appear in shock, as he had claimed, on the morning after the accident.

This information gave Teddy the upper hand. Knowing the prosecution's case beforehand would allow him to orchestrate his answers to fit the facts, Damore claims. "He knew even before he went into that inquest what questions they were going to ask," Damore said recently. The defense would get no unpleasant surprises.

Six months after Mary Jo Kopechne died, the inquest was held in an old New England courthouse in Edgartown on Martha's Vineyard. It ended three days later after testimony from the senator and 26 other witnesses. The judge who handled the case found "probable cause" that Ted's negligence had contributed to Kopechne's death.

No Autopsy on Kopechne's Body

The body of Mary Jo Kopechne was flown from Massachusetts to her hometown in Pennsylvania, where she was buried under a simple grave marker.

In the months prior to the inquest, the District Attorney's office came forward with a claim that blood was found on Kopechne's mouth and nose. An autopsy on her body was ordered, despite protests from Kopechne's parents, Gwen and Joseph, who were later to receive a $140,000 settlement from the senator's insurance company.

Since her death, rumors had circulated that Kopechne was pregnant at the time of the accident. Her parents were under the impression the autopsy was ordered primarily to determine if that was true.

The Kopechnes' attorneys fought a tough case against the prosecutors who wanted the woman's grave opened. In the end, they succeeded; Kopechne's body would not be exhumed. No one would ever know whether she died of asphyxiation from lack of air or whether she drowned in the salty sea water as her death certificate states.

The issue of her pregnancy also would remain murky. A chemical analysis of the slacks she wore on the night of her death was inconclusive. Her clothing was later burned, allegedly at the insistence of her parents.

The Lingering Aftermath

When the inquest judge failed to indict Ted after finding probable cause to believe his negligence contributed to Kopechne's death, the foreman of the Edgartown grand jury, Les Leland, issued a call for a grand jury investigation. On April 6, 1970, Leland convened the grand jury to look into the case. One day later, after calling just four witnesses, the case against the senator was closed. No indictment was ever returned.

Twenty years later, Leland charged that the grand jury proceedings were a farce and a cover-up.

"I know (now) that there was a cover-up going on," Leland said in a 1989 interview. "As I look back, I realize a lot of manipulation went on. Everyone was concerned about protecting Ted Kennedy's political career and to hell that this young girl met a tragic death."

For 22 years, Teddy has continued to maintain that he was not involved in any attempts to cover up his actions on the night of July 18, 1969, and has said no attempt was made to manipulate the investigation into the accident.

The tragedy of that night has continued to haunt the senator's political life. Because of it, he is likely never to

Joseph and Gwen Kopechne fought to prevent an autopsy on their daughter.

sit in the White House. A test run at the 1980 presidential election fell through under the lingering cloud of Chappaquiddick. In a way, the tragedy has given him new measure in his life. It has removed from him the pressure of attaining the presidency and following in his older brother's footsteps.

For Gwen and Joseph Kopechne, Mary Jo's parents, that is little relief. In a 1989 interview with *Ladies' Home Journal,* one of the few interviews they have given since Chappaquiddick, the Kopechnes said the only time they have spoken to the senator since their daughter's death was when he phoned while campaigning in Pennsylvania for the presidency.

But the lingering questions they have for him remain unanswered. "I want him to tell me what happened," Mrs. Kopechne said in that article. "Can't he relieve us of this? Isn't there something he could tell me that would lift this heavy, heavy burden from my heart?" Apparently not. The Senator's offices in Boston and Washington have refused all comment on Chappaquiddick.

Unraveling the Mystery

Syndicated columnist Jack Anderson (above) wrote that unnamed sources charged Kennedy with orchestrating a cover-up of the accident that claimed the life of Mary Jo Kopechne. The unexplained mysteries of Chappaquiddick were instrumental in Teddy Kennedy's failed bid for the presidency in 1980 (opposite). In addition, several speeches had shown him performing poorly, and his estranged wife, Joan, was not looking well. A crushing defeat in the Iowa caucuses proved that his family name was not enough to give him the presidency. He later said that he had learned to lose— a hard lesson for a Kennedy.

Like the assassination of his brother John, the mystery surrounding Ted's behavior at Chappaquiddick has fueled conspiracy theorists.

Shortly after the accident, syndicated columnist Jack Anderson, citing unnamed sources, wrote that Teddy, hoping to save his presidential dream, had decided to ask his cousin and fellow party-goer, Joe Gargan, to take the rap for him. Anderson said he believed Gargan and another friend, Paul Markham, got a boat and took Teddy across the small channel to Edgartown to get him away from the accident scene and help him establish an alibi. In fact, about 2:30 A.M. Kennedy went out and asked the hotel night clerk what time it was. But the next morning after his car was found, Teddy had a change of heart and went to the police.

In the first book on the accident, *The Bridge at Chappaquiddick,* by Jack Olsen, the author theorized that Teddy got out of the car because he feared being caught with a woman after a police officer spotted him and Kopechne driving along. Olsen claims that Kopechne, driving alone and slightly intoxicated on the unfamiliar island, drove the car off Dike Bridge herself. Kennedy, he postulates, was forced to stick to his story after giving a statement to police.

In a 1971 book, *Teddy Bare: The Last of the Kennedy Clan,* author Zad Rust claims Teddy jumped from the moving car before it went into the water and then conspired with higher forces to cover up the accident to protect the senator's presidential dream.

In *Death at Chappaquiddick,* by Richard and Thomas Tedrow, the authors theorize that, unbeknownst to the senator, Kopechne was asleep in the back seat when he took the car to the last ferry out of Chappaquiddick.

In *Chappaquiddick Revealed,* Kenneth Kappel builds on the evidence uncovered by previous writers and studies the photos of the damage to the Oldsmobile. Because the side of the car is damaged, Kappel believes that the accident to the car occurred before the car went into the water. His theory is that Kennedy, who had been drinking, was driving Kopechne and had an accident in which the car went off the road and hit some trees. Kopechne was injured and knocked into a coma. Kennedy went to fetch Grogan and Markham, and the three of them, believing Kopechne dead and beyond help, pushed the Oldsmobile off the bridge and into Poucha Pond.

Perhaps the wildest theory, however, comes from conspiracy proponent R. B. Cutler, who claims that outsiders, in a bid to keep Teddy out of the White House, injected Kopechne with alcohol, damaged the senator's car, and then, using a look-alike, drove his car off Dike Bridge.

WIVES AND WIDOWS: THE KENNEDY WOMEN

The day after John F. Kennedy was elected president, the Kennedy clan posed in Hyannis Port for this family picture. Those seated, left to right, are Eunice Shriver, family matriarch Rose Kennedy, patriarch Joe Kennedy, Jackie Kennedy, and Teddy Kennedy. Standing, left to right, are Ethel Kennedy, Stephen Smith, Jean Kennedy Smith, Jack Kennedy, Bobby Kennedy, Patricia Lawford, R. Sargent Shriver, Joan Kennedy, and Peter Lawford.

Jackie Kennedy Onassis

Even as early as 1947, Jackie Bouvier (right) was known for her beauty and style. While working as an inquiring photographer (below), she caught the eye of John F. Kennedy, the handsome senator from Massachusetts.

Jacqueline Lee Bouvier grew up amid the opulent lifestyle of Newport and East Hampton high society. The daughter of stockbroker John "Black Jack" Bouvier and socialite Janet Lee, she was raised in privileged circles, learning a love of the fine arts and of horses that she has carried with her throughout her 63 years.

But her early life was far from settled. Her father, a notorious gambler, squandered away much of the family's fortune. Her parents' divorce when she was nearly 11 years old left both her and her younger sister, Lee, shattered. It also helped form her tough, no-nonsense character.

In 1951, Jackie, an attractive inquiring photographer for the old *Washington Times-Herald,* caught the eye of the new senator from Massachusetts, Jack Kennedy, at a Washington dinner party. They were married two years later on September 12, 1953, at St. Mary's Church in Newport, Rhode Island, with more than 3,000 curious spectators gathered outside.

The two attractive young people had a far from storybook marriage. Jackie had a miscarriage in 1955; a year later, she had an emergency cesarean in which a second child, a girl, was stillborn.

Two years after Jackie met Jack Kennedy, on September 12, 1953, the belle of Rhode Island high society and the most eligible bachelor in Washington were married in an elaborate ceremony in Newport, Rhode Island (above).

Then in November 1957, Jackie gave birth to a healthy, seven-pound baby girl, which the new parents christened Caroline Bouvier Kennedy. In November 1960, between her husband's election to the presidency and his inauguration, a pregnant Jackie prematurely delivered a baby boy they named John Fitzgerald Kennedy, Jr.

Three years later, on August 7, 1963, a second son, Patrick Bouvier Kennedy, was delivered by cesarean. Born five weeks premature and weighing less than five pounds, the little baby suffered serious respiratory problems. He died two days later.

Outwardly, Jackie feigned ignorance of her husband's affairs.

In 1961, Jackie accompanied her husband to Paris to visit French President Charles de Gaulle (left) and was met by adoring crowds. Europeans and Americans alike were captivated by her elegance and stylishness. For a state dinner at Versailles (below), she wore a full-length silk coat over a Givenchy gown—her husband, with less élan, carried a fedora with his dress suit. The same sense of class she brought to fashion showed through in her restoration of the White House. Jackie served as guide on a national television program (opposite, top) showcasing the remodeled executive mansion. She is shown with CBS-TV correspondent Charles Collingwood (opposite, bottom) in the refurbished Monroe Cabinet Room. Her efforts turned the presidential home into a national monument filled with more than $10 million in priceless antiques and historical artifacts.

Her Wandering Husband

Jackie's childbearing problems were nothing compared to the humiliation caused by her husband's roving eye. According to Kitty Kelley's best-selling biography *Jackie Oh!*, Jack started romancing one of his secretaries, Pamela Turnure, not long after their marriage. Later, after Jack was elected president, Jackie hired Turnure as her press secretary—apparently knowing full well that her husband was having an affair with the young woman. One theory holds that Jackie wanted to make Jack's indiscretions so easy that he would become bored.

Jackie's husband found ways to continue his sexual forays when he became president. Nude swimming parties in the White House pool and sexual conquests in the Lincoln Bedroom were amongst his pastimes. Like Rose Kennedy, Jackie learned to live with the knowledge of her husband's infidelity.

Jackie's Spending Sprees

Outwardly, Jackie feigned ignorance of her husband's affairs. She turned her interests toward restoring the White House, a project that her taste and knowledge of art and antiques suited her for. She spent several hundred thousand dollars on the restoration.

Her lavish spending was legendary. *Women's Wear Daily,* in an article published prior to the 1960 election, reported that Jackie spent $30,000 a year on clothing alone. She denied the charge, saying, "I couldn't spend that much unless I wore sable underwear." But her spending upset her husband, wealthy as he was. As first lady, her personal expenses for one year included $40,000 for clothing, $900 for riding accessories, and another $800 for a vacuum cleaner for her horses.

During JFK's first two years in office, she spent a total of $226,907.75—$26,907.75 more than her husband made as president during that time, and Kennedy donated his salary to charity.

Dr. Feelgood

Amphetamines, or "speed," were thought at the time to be harmless.

Jackie was an enormous success on the trip to France (above). Even before the trip, the president and his wife had consulted with Dr. Max Jacobson (left). The "speed" he administered helped Jack and Jackie through their exhausting schedule in France, such as attending the ballet performance with de Gaulle at Versailles (opposite, bottom). After her husband's assassination, Jackie leaned heavily on his brother, Bobby (opposite, top), sparking rumors of a romance.

Jackie's first experience with drugs began innocently enough. Her husband was concerned about his wife's depression and the severe headaches she suffered since the birth of John Junior. Jack called on New York physician Max Jacobson, known to his patients as "Dr. Feelgood," and whom Jack had known about since his campaign in 1960. Jack explained that Jackie was about to accompany him to Canada and needed something to help her through the long round of scheduled events. Jacobson gave Jackie a shot for her migraine, and within minutes, she was feeling better.

Jacobson was again called to Washington by the president to help him and Jackie prepare for their first trip to Europe. He treated the first couple for four days and then flew with them to France.

Jacobson was injecting the president and his wife with an amphetamine and steroid mix. Amphetamines, or "speed," were thought at the time to be harmless. According to C. David Heymann's book *A Woman Named Jackie*, by the time the president and his wife left on the state visit to Europe, both were already mildly addicted to the amphetamine and steroid mix Jacobson was prescribing.

Soon after their return to Washington, "the Kennedys began using the services of Jacobson on a regular basis, at least once a week and occasionally as often as three and four times weekly," Heymann writes. "By the summer of 1961, they had both developed a strong dependence on amphetamines."

Jacobson served as unofficial doctor to the first couple through the remainder of Camelot, giving JFK his last injection on November 15, 1963—just a week before that fateful day in Dallas.

Jackie's Search for Privacy

Jack's assassination, coming three months after the loss of her second son, Patrick, devastated Jackie and created a whole new set of problems for the president's widow. The press dogged her every move. Busloads of tourists gawked at her house in Washington's prestigious Georgetown section.

Soon she gathered up her children and moved to a five-bedroom apartment on New York's Fifth Avenue, where she hoped to achieve the anonymity she craved. Hoping to protect her children from prying eyes, she enrolled them in private schools. Later, she began undergoing psycho-analysis in an attempt to deal with the latest tragedy. And she leaned heavily on her husband's brother, Bobby. This sparked rumors of an affair, much to the dismay of Bobby's wife, Ethel.

Hounded by Paparazzi

Candid photos of Jackie were published in magazines and newspapers around the world.

Years after her husband's death, the public's intense interest in Jackie made the former first lady one of the most photographed woman in the world—and photographer Ron Galella one of her more relentless pursuers. While she walked down New York's Madison Avenue wearing her trademark sunglasses (below), *Galella was snapping away from behind.*

But New York was not much different from Washington. As Jackie eased back into the social scene, gossip columnists recorded her every move. Photographers hounded her every step. Among them was paparazzo Ron Galella, whose candid photos of Jackie were published in magazines and newspapers around the world.

So relentless was Galella in his pursuit of Jackie and her children that in 1969 his distraught subject had him arrested by Secret Service agents. Citing "grievous mental anguish," she won a permanent injunction against the photographer that ordered him to keep 25 feet away from her and 30 feet away from her children. Galella countersued for $1.3 million, claiming "false arrest, malicious persecution and interference with my livelihood as a photographer." His suit was dismissed.

Jackie again sued Galella in 1981, when he violated the injunction. She won a $10,000 settlement from him and a court order prohibiting him from ever taking another photograph of her. But Galella's European counterparts exacted a revenge of sorts. Wearing scuba diving gear and carrying underwater cameras, they photographed Jackie and new husband Aristotle Onassis sunbathing nude on the Greek island of Skorpios. The pictures eventually appeared in tabloids and magazines around the world— even in the skin publications *Screw* and *Hustler*.

"...grievous mental anguish..."

At times fashionable, at times disguised, Jackie was never far from Ron Galella's probing lens. He captured her wearing a Valentino dress (top, left) as she left the 21 Club in New York in 1980. He found her leaving her son's school (top, right) hiding behind sunglasses and a scarf. He caught her in Los Angeles lunching (left) in a loose-fitting top and pants.

Christina thought Jackie was a gold digger out for her father's billions.

Husband Number Two

After the proper year of mourning following her husband's death, Jackie began immersing herself in the jet-set lifestyle. Soon her name was linked with a number of admirers—among them politician Adlai Stevenson; Sir David Ormsby-Gore, also known as Lord Harlech, the former British ambassador to the United States; and writer Pete Hamill.

Jackie shocked the world with her 1968 marriage to Greek shipping tycoon Aristotle Onassis (above). But her second marriage was not destined to be a happy one. Onassis's children, Alexander (opposite, left) and Christina (opposite, right) suspected she married their father for his money. Christina is shown here at Studio 54, one of New York's chic clubs in 1977.

On June 5, 1968, Jackie's world fell apart again when her beloved brother-in-law Bobby was shot to death after giving a victory speech at the Ambassador Hotel following the California primary. In her grief over Bobby's death, Jackie turned to Greek billionaire Aristotle Onassis, an old family friend.

Throughout that summer, Onassis visited Jackie constantly. Soon, they were talking marriage. On October 20, 1968, nearly five years after the assassination of her husband, Jackie wed Onassis on the tiny Greek island of Skorpios while her ten-year-old daughter and seven-year-old son looked on.

Family Problems

Onassis's daughter, Christina, never really accepted her new stepmother, whom she termed "The Black Widow." Christina thought Jackie was a gold digger out for her father's billions. Her suspicions were indeed well founded. Jackie could drop $100,000 in ten minutes on a buying spree that could include anything from shoes and furs to the same silk blouse bought in quantity and in a rainbow of colors, according to Heymann's book on the former first lady.

Her prenuptial agreement included a $3-million up-front payment plus the interest on $1-million trust funds for each child until they each turned 21. If the marriage were terminated by divorce or Onassis's death, Jackie would receive $200,000 per year for life. This provision was later changed.

Spoiled and indulged as a child, Christina turned into an awkward, obese young woman

dependent on tranquilizers to control her depressions and amphetamines to control her weight. Having Jackie Kennedy as a stepmother, with her stylish clothes and social graces, was unbearable to Christina. Jackie tried to please the unaccepting Christina, taking her clothes shopping, instructing her on her diet, and inviting her to meet Jackie's New York society friends. But Christina resented her new stepmother all the more.

Onassis's son, Alexander, also despised Jackie, referring openly to her as "the courtesan." Tragedy engulfed the fragile family when Alexander was killed in an airplane crash on January 21, 1973. As a result of Alexander's death, Christina slid into a deep depression that culminated in a suicide attempt that was unsuccessful. After her father's death in 1975, she ran the family shipping business. On November 19, 1988, Christina died suddenly at the age of 37.

The Price for Privacy

At the funeral service for Aristotle Onassis (above), Christina Onassis, in the center, was accompanied by family members. Jackie, widowed a second time, was escorted by her son, John, at the left. Onassis had resumed his relationship with diva Maria Callas (left) shortly after he married Jackie. Today Jackie has a long-time private relationship with New York gem dealer Maurice Templesman (opposite, top). Onassis's death left Jackie $26 million richer, some of which she used to build an expansive retreat on the coast of Martha's Vineyard (opposite, bottom).

Onassis had gradually been drawing away from Jackie and had resumed his relationship with his ex-lover, opera diva Maria Callas. With his son's death and his daughter's attempted suicide, Onassis withdrew from Jackie even further. Bitter over her lavish spending and jet-set lifestyle, Onassis began contemplating divorce. But the marriage was to end instead in Onassis's death on March 15, 1975. His daughter Christina was by his side. His wife of seven years was 3,000 miles away in New York.

Since becoming a widow for a second time, Jackie has maintained a low profile. She works as a book editor for Viking Press and Doubleday Books and attends social events with Maurice Templesman, a married diamond merchant. Jackie's settlement at Onassis's death was $26 million, and Templesman's astute advice has helped her increase her wealth considerably. At last she has the privacy and security she valued.

Ethel Skakel Kennedy

Surrounded by nine of their ten children, Robert and Ethel Kennedy pose for a family portrait (above). An 11th child, Rory, was born after her father's death. In recent years, Ethel has led a low-key lifestyle. In a rare appearance (opposite, bottom), she attended the wedding of her niece Maria Shriver to Arnold Schwarzenegger in Hyannis.

Ethel Skakel met Bobby Kennedy in 1944 while skiing in Canada. Their relationship bloomed, and they married six years later. An energetic, outgoing, strong woman, she is the mother of a brood that eventually totaled 11. Ethel also was the political fire keeper for many of her husband's campaigns.

She was no stranger to tragedy. She had lived through the deaths of both her parents, George and Ann Skakel, who were killed when their plane crashed after taking off from Tulsa, Oklahoma, in 1955. Ten years after that accident, Ethel's brother George was killed in a plane crash along with four others. The group had chartered a Cessna to fly them to an elk hunt, and the plane crashed in Idaho. Just a brief 18 months later, Ethel was again attending a funeral—this time for George's wife, who choked to death on a piece of meat during an informal dinner at her Greenwich, Connecticut, home.

Still more tragedy was to follow.

The Mystery of Martha Moxley

On the night before Halloween in 1975, 15-year-old Martha Moxley, a classmate of Ethel's 17-year-old nephew, Thomas Skakel, was found bludgeoned to death just 200 feet from her home in the exclusive Belle Haven section of Greenwich, Connecticut. Thomas, who lived right across the street, was the last to see the pretty, blue-eyed blonde alive. The murder weapon, a golf club, came from a set belonging to the Skakel family. Tom Skakel passed a lie-detector test, but within several weeks of the killing he stopped cooperating with the police. His father refused police requests for a full psychiatric examination of the teenager. Later, Tom was sent to stay in Ireland, which got him away from police questioning. People in the community had the idea that Kennedy influence had helped in insulating Thomas Skakel.

Martha's killer was never found. Police, however, recently said they are considering reopening the investigation into Martha's death and the possible role of Ethel's nephew.

Life After Bobby

After her husband's death, Ethel lived a relatively quiet life at the family's Hickory Hill home in Virginia, raising her brood of 11 with the help of nannies, housekeepers, and social secretaries. Many of these employees quit because of Ethel's difficult temper. Unable to tighten the reigns on her spirited children, many of them ran wild, living up to their self-imposed sobriquet "the Hyannis Port Terrors." For many of the youngsters, the pressures of living up to their father's image became a difficult, if not impossible, task. To compensate, some of them turned to drugs.

Ethel Kennedy, who once considered becoming a nun, has found strength in her Catholic faith to weather a lifetime of tragedies and scandals. She still attends church regularly and encourages her children to do the same. Her husband's memory remains vivid in her mind, and she constantly works to uphold his dreams, often attending functions that promote his philosophy.

Despite the claims of an affair between Bobby and Marilyn Monroe, Ethel has never taken those rumors seriously, preferring instead to idolize him in death as she did in life.

Guardedly secret in her private life, she was linked in the mid-1970s with two men—Canadian lawyer William J. vanden Heuvel, a friend and former aide to her husband, and Warren Rogers, Jr., a widower and bureau chief for now-defunct *Look* magazine. Nothing ever came of those relationships, probably because of both her religious upbringing and her still-deep feelings for Bobby. Years after his death, friends recalled that she was appalled when they suggested she find someone else. "How could I possibly do that with Bobby looking down from heaven? That would be adultery," she said.

Joan Bennett Kennedy

Virginia Joan Bennett seemed to have it all. An attractive, blonde debutante and model, she was a student at Manhattanville College in New York when she was introduced to Edward Moore Kennedy by his sister Jean, who also attended the school. A year after that first meeting, the former college queen and the dashing young law student were married on November 29, 1958, by family friend Francis Cardinal Spellman.

"Politics took over our lives almost immediately," she recalled in Marcia Chellis's unauthorized biography, *Living with the Kennedys: The Joan Kennedy Story*. Soon motherhood took over from politics. A daughter, Kara, was born in 1960. A son, Teddy Junior, followed in 1961. In May 1963, Joan suffered her first miscarriage. A year later, she lost another child in her fourth month of pregnancy. Her second son, Patrick, was born in 1967. She was in her third month of pregnancy when she again miscarried during the height of the publicity surrounding her husband's car accident at Chappaquiddick.

Rumors of Teddy's infidelities circulated to Joan, who at first refused to believe them.

A stunningly attractive Joan Bennett (above) seemed the perfect political wife when she married Edward Kennedy in 1958 (left). She campaigned vigorously for her husband's election to the Senate (opposite, top), never hesitating to give campaign speeches on her husband's behalf. Privately, she was a doting mother to her children (opposite, bottom). But the life of a politician's wife also came with a price. Joan, apparently aware of her husband's philandering, chose to ignore it and to try to maintain a normal home life for herself and her children.

Ted's Womanizing Takes its Toll

Joan's husband, like his father and brothers before him, found himself attracted to other women almost immediately after his marriage. Rumors of Teddy's infidelities circulated to Joan, who at first refused to believe them.

But her suspicions were confirmed during the Chappaquiddick affair. A pregnant Joan was staying in Hyannis Port when the Chappaquiddick saga began to unfold. Joan can still recall picking up a telephone extension at the family's compound and hearing Ted tell his girlfriend, Helga Wagner, about the accident.

"It was a terrible experience, one of the worst in my life," she later told Chellis. "And it was the beginning of the end for Ted and me."

Soon Teddy became even more indiscreet in his relationships. He conducted a highly publicized affair with Amanda Burden, a beautiful, 28-year-old former aide to his brother Bobby and the daughter of William S. Paley, the chairman of the board at CBS. A long list of women followed. Joan turned to alcohol, rather than her husband, for comfort.

The Lure of Alcohol

With Ted often away from home, Joan became lonely, depressed, and overwhelmed with feelings of inadequacy. She became a binge drinker. To overcome her feelings, she tried having an affair of her own, but that too ended in failure when her prospective lover went to her hotel room and found her drunk. On other occasions, she would hop a plane to some far-off destination, only to be fetched home by a family friend.

By 1974, unable to cope with her drinking problem, Joan entered a monthlong treatment program in New Canaan, Connecticut. It didn't work. Not long after her release, she was stopped for drunk driving near her Virginia home and ordered to undergo alcohol rehabilitation. As soon as she returned home from that treatment program, she hit the bottle again.

In 1978, after a year of self-imposed sobriety, Joan went public with her problem in an article for *McCall's* magazine. Even though the article won her wide praise, Joan had a relapse not long after it hit the newsstands.

Two very public drunk driving arrests put Joan's alcohol problems back in the spotlight. In 1988, she struck a fence on Cape Cod. Three years later, in May 1991, she was again stopped while driving drunk in Quincy, Massachusetts, just miles from her Boston home. She had an open bottle of vodka in her car. She pleaded guilty to a drunk driving charge and was ordered once again to undergo alcohol rehabilitation.

Joan's alcoholism was a family secret, hushed up by the Kennedy political machine. But in 1974, it became public news after she was arrested for drunken driving (above) *near her home in McLean, Virginia. In 1988* (opposite, left) *and 1991* (left), *she was arrested and charged with drunken driving again. Joan campaigned with Teddy when he decided to run for president in 1980* (opposite, right), *but after he dropped out, the marriage disintegrated.*

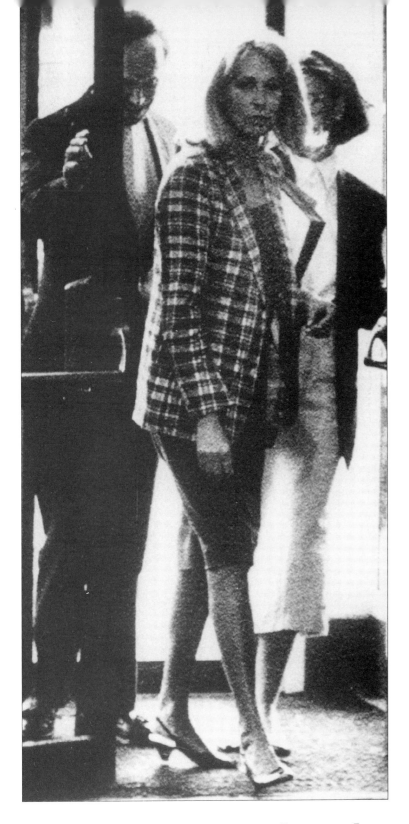

Joan became lonely, depressed.

The End of a Marriage

Despite her husband's womanizing and the humiliation of Chappaquiddick, Joan stood solidly by him, campaigning tirelessly for Teddy's reelection to the Senate. By 1973, however, stories began to appear that Joan and Ted had reached an unofficial agreement to lead separate lives. Three years later, the stories were confirmed when Joan moved into an apartment on Beacon Street in Boston's trendy Back Bay neighborhood. She kept herself occupied by getting a graduate degree in music education, attending the theater and social events, and working with the Boston Pops and the Symphony orchestras.

When Ted decided to campaign for president in 1979, Joan was back at his side, the faithful wife of a faithless husband. She campaigned for him relentlessly during the winter of that year, flying across the country to attend political functions. But the reconciliation didn't last. One month after Teddy dropped out of the race, they became legally separated.

Months later, according to an account by Chellis, Joan strode into her husband's den. "How are you going to handle the questions?" she asked him, "because I want a divorce."

The fairy-tale marriage of Joan and Ted was at an end.

Eunice Kennedy Shriver

Eunice Kennedy has long been considered the best and the brightest of Joseph P. Kennedy's daughters. "If that girl had been born with balls," he once said, "she would have been a hell of a politician." He intended the remark as a compliment.

Eunice was a top student at Stanford University. She did social work in Harlem and West Virginia and later worked for both the State and Justice Departments. A spirited campaigner for her politician brothers, she also curried a number of friendships with prominent individuals—among them Wisconsin Senator Joseph McCarthy, whom she once dated.

It was Sargent Shriver, however, who won her heart. They married in 1953 after a seven-year courtship. For Eunice, Shriver was a man cut from her father's mold. "I searched all my life for someone like my father and Sarge came closest," she said in her wedding toast to him.

Indeed, Shriver entered the Kennedys' political realm with gusto, becoming the first director of the Peace Corps under JFK and, later, the U.S. Ambassador to France.

***Sargent and Eunice Shriver* (right) *were all smiles at the wedding of their daughter Maria to strongman actor Arnold Schwarzenegger* (below).**

A Successful Family

While her husband made the political rounds, Eunice took great care in raising the couple's five children, Robert, Maria, Timothy, Mark, and Anthony. She made a special effort to keep them away from their more troublesome cousins. Political discussions at the dinner table were common in the Shriver home, where Eunice often taped newsworthy articles to the dining-room mantel. Her efforts apparently paid off. All five of her children have taken up the family's tradition for public service.

Eunice also took up the family challenge. Her closeness to her mentally retarded sister, Rosemary, led her to start a day camp for the mentally retarded in the backyard of her Rockville, Maryland, home in 1963. Five years later, in 1968, she started the Special Olympics. In 1957, she began directing the Joseph P. Kennedy, Jr., Foundation for the mentally retarded. She has supported this organization for more than 30 years.

Eunice has avoided the notoriety that seems to plague her kinfolk. Nowadays she gets as much attention for being the mother-in-law of Arnold Schwarzenegger as she does for being a Kennedy. The actor—a staunch Republican—married her daughter, Maria, in an elaborate Hyannis Port wedding in 1988.

Jean Kennedy Smith

The eighth of Joseph and Rose Kennedy's nine children, Jean Kennedy Smith has long been considered the least demanding of all the Kennedy women. Tirelessly committed to raising funds for charity, she is looked upon by outsiders as sophisticated, kind, and among the least troubled in the family.

But like the other Kennedy women, Jean has had her share of problems. After marrying Stephen Smith, a wealthy New York businessman, in 1956, Jean turned her interests toward raising her sons Stephen Junior and Willie and her adopted daughters Amanda and Kym.

Her husband, however, developed other interests. As the "family fixer," Smith was well known for his astute handling of any personal or political problems the Kennedy brothers found themselves involved in. He also became notorious for skirt chasing. "He literally had one girl to his left and another to his right," a family acquaintance told *People* magazine.

Her husband's carousing prompted Jean to have an affair of her own with an Italian, but he spurned her. After that, Smith's attitude toward his wife became even worse. "He treated her like dirt," the acquaintance is quoted as saying.

Jean Kennedy Smith at home with two of her four children, William, 2, and Stephen, 5 (above). Though her husband was a known womanizer, she maintained the role of dignified widow at her husband's funeral (inset), where she was escorted by her son Willie.

Soon, the couple began living apart. "She just withered from within," a close friend told *People*. "Her pain was so great that she stopped venturing out into the world."

After her husband was diagnosed with lung cancer in 1987, the couple reconciled. She nursed him at home and traveled with the family to Europe before Smith died in 1989.

It stunned Jean when her son Willie, who had no prior arrest record, was charged with rape shortly after March 30, 1991. Following the family tradition, Jean continues to steadfastly support her son, despite statements from three other women who recently came forward with similar stories about him.

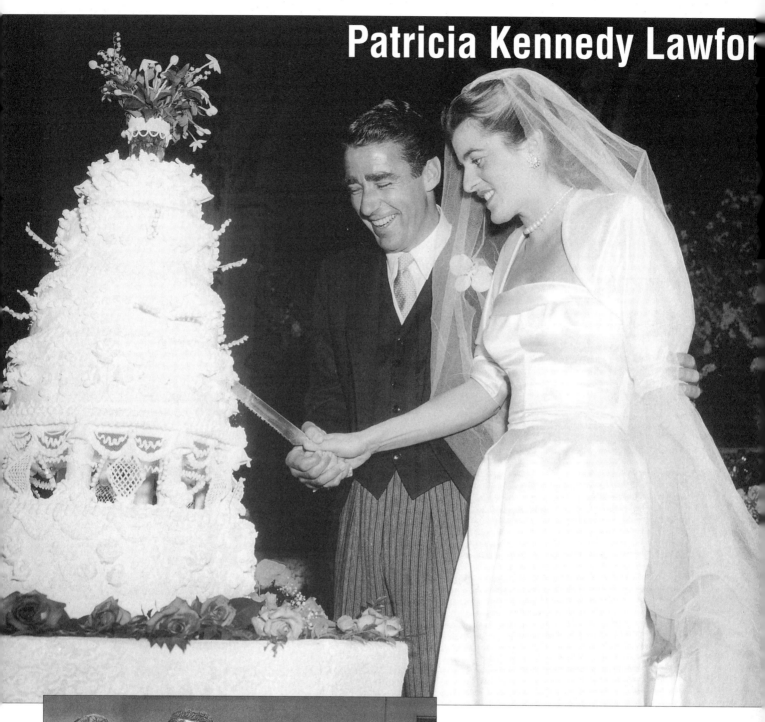

Because Patricia Kennedy had always been in awe of movie stars, it wasn't surprising that she fell for one. Peter Lawford was just a contract player for MGM when Pat first met him in 1949 at the home of Gary Cooper. They met again in 1952, and soon Pat was in love.

Her father objected to the romance, at one point telling Lawford: "If there's anything I'd hate as a son-in-law, it's an actor; and if there's anything I think I'd hate worse than an actor as a son-in-law, it's an English actor." But Lawford was not deterred. After converting to Catholicism, he married Pat in 1954. Their first child, Christopher, was born the following year. His birth was soon followed by those of his three sisters, Sydney, Victoria, and Robin.

But the Lawford marriage was troubled from the start. The actor was a notorious womanizer and playboy who hung out with Frank Sinatra's fun-loving "Rat Pack"—a group of entertainers who loved to party together.

As her marriage crumbled, Pat cloaked her sorrow in a dangerous mix of pills and alcohol. Her brother Jack asked her to postpone any talk of divorce until after the 1964 election, fearing it would harm his political chances. Pat agreed.

But her brother was assassinated in 1963. Shortly thereafter, Pat packed her bags, gathered up her children, and fled the couple's California home for New York. In violation of her Catholic beliefs, Pat filed for divorce citing "mental cruelty." The divorce came through in 1966. Eighteen years later, Peter Lawford died of cardiac failure and complications of cirrhosis.

Life After Divorce

Pat Lawford's problems didn't end with her divorce from her husband of 12 years. Her only son, Christopher, has been arrested several times on drug charges.

Since her well-publicized divorce, Pat has led a quiet, almost reclusive life. In a recent profile of her in *People* magazine, a longtime friend said that outside of her family "no one sees her anymore." The only publicity surrounding her came in 1989, when police stopped her on Long Island after hitting a utility pole. She pleaded guilty to a charge of driving while impaired.

Despite the objections of her father, Patricia Kennedy married actor Peter Lawford (opposite, top) in a storybook wedding in 1954. But the storybook marriage soon turned stormy. Lawford was one of Hollywood's swinging "Rat Pack" with Dean Martin, Sammy Davis Jr., and Frank Sinatra (opposite, bottom). Patricia is shown (below) in a Santa Monica, California, courtroom awaiting sentencing for driving with an expired driver's license.

David's Demise

The demons that alcohol conjured up in the older generation were passed on to the younger members of the Kennedy family with a far deadlier addiction—drugs. Cocaine, heroin, marijuana, and downers—all chosen to ease the pain of a generation raised amid opulence and tragedy—became the drugs of choice for the younger members of the clan.

For David, the son of Robert and Ethel, the combination of drugs and booze proved to be a fatal mix. Sensitive and somewhat introspective, David never really fit into the family image. He was, to many in the family, the black sheep of the clan. Perhaps it was seeing his father's assassination on television as a 12-year-old that drove him deeper into himself. Perhaps it was the challenge of living up to the Kennedy image. Regardless of which inner demons drove him to despair, by the time he reached his 23rd birthday, David was a full-blown junkie.

From 1977 to 1979, while undergoing psychiatric treatment for his problems, David became addicted to the prescription drugs Percodan, Dilaudid, and Quaalude. During a single 18-month period, a Cambridge, Massachusetts, psychiatrist who was treating David at the time wrote him 50 prescriptions for those drugs.

By 1979, David's addiction drove him to comb the sleazy streets of New York City's drug underworld, looking for the ultimate fix. One night, in a run-down hotel frequented by drug addicts, police found him the apparent victim of a mugging. Not long after, he was hospitalized for six weeks at Massachusetts General Hospital in Boston, where he was treated for bacterial endocarditis, a heart ailment sometimes associated with drug addiction. In 1980, David had his second skirmish with the law when he was arrested in Sacramento, California, and charged with drunk driving.

By the spring of 1984, 28-year-old David's long slide into drug and alcohol addiction was nearing an end.

After leaving a Minneapolis detox center where he had spent the previous month trying to kick his drug and booze problem, David flew to the Kennedy estate in Palm Beach. It was expected to be a final reunion with his ailing grandmother, Rose Kennedy, who had had a stroke and was considered close to death at the time.

But it was David who died, troubled and alone, that Easter weekend, after a five-day binge of booze and pills.

By the time he reached his 23rd birthday, David was a full-blown junkie.

The black sheep of the family, David Kennedy was a hard-core junkie by the time he was in his early 20s (opposite and right). In 1980, he was living in Sacramento, California, and under the care of a drug counselor (above).

A Life Gone Wrong

David's final days were spent snorting cocaine and downing double vodkas at Palm Beach night spots and beside the pool at the posh Brazilian Court Hotel, where on April 25, 1984, hotel workers found his lifeless body lying on the floor between two beds.

An autopsy found he died from a deadly combination of liquid Demerol, the tranquilizer Mellaril, and ultrapure cocaine.

David's death sparked many unanswered questions.

A medical examiner's report released later said that Kennedy had been turned away from the family's beachfront estate when he turned up "drunk or stoned."

Newspapers later reported that one of the three drugs found in his body—liquid Demerol—had been stolen from his ailing grandmother during a visit with her two days earlier.

Investigators also suspected that someone had entered David's room after his death and disposed of drugs in an effort to cover up the cause of his death. An analysis of water from his bathroom toilet, in fact, showed traces of cocaine and Demerol, leading authorities to believe someone had flushed the drugs down the toilet.

Among the police's suspects were David's young cousins Caroline Kennedy and Sydney Lawford McKelvy. Both had been seen near his room 90 minutes before Ethel Kennedy placed a call to hotel management asking them to check on her son. Investigators' suspicions were bolstered when an unnamed person came forward to allege that Caroline and Sydney had admitted taking two syringes and cocaine from his room before his death was discovered.

Both Kennedy cousins later denied the allegations in interviews with police.

During Easter weekend in 1984, David was staying at the Brazilian Court Hotel (opposite). *Kennedy lawyers tried unsuccessfully to stop the release of photos of the room where David died (above). At the right is the bathroom where authorities believe someone flushed cocaine and Demerol down the toilet in an effort to hide the cause of death. Among the police's chief suspects for this act were David's cousins Caroline Kennedy and Sydney Lawford McKelvy, both of whom had been seen near his room shortly before his death was discovered. David's body (left) was returned to his family for burial.*

Heroin's Hold over Young Bobby

David's death shattered the tightly knit clan but did little to stop his older brother Robert, Jr., from dabbling in the hazy netherworld of heroin.

His fling with drugs began innocently enough with marijuana. As a 16-year-old in 1970, he and his cousin Robert Sargent Shriver III were arrested in Hyannis Port for possession of the drug. It was a minor rap for a juvenile but one that came with a year's probation.

For the next 13 years, Bobby kept clear of major trouble, following the political path laid out for him by his family. But by the age of 29, the pressures of living up to his father's image combined with his failure to pass the New York bar exam caught up with him.

Until 1983, Bobby appeared, to outsiders at least, free of the demons that plagued his younger brother. At the time, few knew that over the previous two years he had developed a $1,000-a-week heroin habit—a habit that had led him, at times, to the seedy haunts of New York City's Spanish Harlem in search of a fix.

On August 3 of that year, a passenger on a Republic Airlines flight to Rapid City, South Dakota, found Bobby sitting inside a lavatory, incoherently asking for help for what was later thought to be a heroin overdose. The pilot radioed ahead for an ambulance, but when the plane touched down, Bobby was feeling better and declined help. Police, however, were suspicious. They detained Bobby for questioning and confiscated his carry-on bag, where they later discovered two-tenths of a gram of heroin.

After pleading guilty to heroin possession, he was placed on two years' probation, completing it successfully in 1986.

Once the bright hope of the next Kennedy generation, Robert F. Kennedy, Jr., shared his father's dreams and ambitions (above). *But by 1981, the pressures of living such a public existance drove him into a $1,000-a-week heroin habit. Recently he has plugged social causes such as the Rose Kennedy social center* (right) *in Brooklyn.*

Drugs Claim a Kennedy Cousin

Christopher Lawford talked with his lawyer in a Boston court (above) *after pleading innocent to possession of heroin in 1980.*

The temptation of drugs was not limited to Robert and Ethel's children.

Christopher Lawford, son of Peter and Patricia Lawford, also had his share of heroin highs—and lows.

His first brush with drugs is documented in 1980, when he was arrested and charged with trying to coerce an Aspen, Colorado, pharmacist into turning over a number of capsules of the painkiller Darvon. The charges were later dropped.

By 1980, Christopher, like his cousin Bobby, had turned to heroin. His arrest record shows he was stopped in Boston in December of that year and charged with heroin possession after police spotted him making a buy outside a bar in a run-down section of the city.

When police stopped the car in which he was riding, Christopher offered no resistance. He emerged with the heroin in his hand. Charges against him were later dropped after he completed a year's probation.

Now an aspiring Hollywood actor, Christopher claims he has been free of his drug dependency for the past five years.

111

Tragedy and the Younger Generation

Tragedy in the lives of the younger generation of Kennedys was fueled by more than drugs. A sense of carelessness, impermeability, perhaps a sense of immortality, and fate resulted in often chilling encounters.

Joseph Patrick Kennedy III, Robert and Ethel's oldest son, steered clear of the pitfalls of drugs but could not escape the family's proclivity for bad luck.

Joseph's first major encounter with fate came in February 1972, when he was on a jumbo jet en route from India to Europe that was hijacked by Arab guerrillas. Initially authorities feared he had been abducted in retaliation for the imprisonment of his father's assassin, Sirhan Sirhan, but this time fate was on his side. He was released unharmed shortly after the hijacking.

Fate wasn't so kind a year later. On August 13, 1973, Joseph and his brother David were on an end-of-summer fling on the island of Nantucket. Joseph was driving a jeep, which flipped over with seven passengers aboard.

One of those passengers, 18-year-old Pamela Kelly, was David Kennedy's girlfriend. She was paralyzed in the crash,

The oldest son of Robert and Ethel Kennedy's 11 children, Joseph Kennedy III has had his share of tragedies. In 1973, he was the driver of a jeep that flipped over on the island of Nantucket with seven young people aboard. He is shown (above) awaiting help following the accident as a nurse tended to one of the injured. Now a U.S. Congressman from Massachusetts, Joe showed off that famous Kennedy smile in a more recent photo (left).

112

which also seriously injured David. While recovering in the hospital from a fractured vertebra, David developed a taste for the morphine doctors used to ease his pain. It was a taste he later satisfied with heroin.

Even those family members who appeared to steer clear of the Kennedy maelstrom were caught up in the web of tragedy.

Edward Kennedy, Jr., the son of the Massachusetts senator, was diagnosed with chondrosarcoma, a fast-growing cancer of the cartilage in November 1973, when he was 12 years old. His right leg had to be amputated above the knee to prevent the cancer from spreading. Four months after that operation, he had rebounded well enough to go skiing with his family in Vail, Colorado.

By 1980, however, 19-year-old Teddy Junior was also dabbling in drugs—he was arrested in New Jersey for possession of marijuana. Eleven years later, he was admitted to a $590-a-day treatment program in Hartford, Connecticut, where he underwent rehabilitation for alcoholism.

Edward Kennedy, Jr., was diagnosed with cancer.

It didn't take long for Teddy Junior to get back on the ski slopes (right) *after losing his right leg to cancer at the age of 12. Today* (above), *Ted bears a striking physical resemblance to his father.*

JFK Junior

Gifted with his father's good looks and charm, John has drawn the notice of a whole new generation of Kennedy admirers, many of whom were not even born when young "John-John" saluted his father's casket as it was taken to Arlington National Cemetery, where the assassinated president was buried on John's third birthday.

As John grew into adulthood, America stood on the sidelines watching in fascination. Like his sister, Caroline, his every move was recorded in the press. By the time he reached 26, John had become known not only for his name, but for his striking good looks. *People* magazine named him "America's Most Eligible Bachelor" that year; in 1988 they dubbed him "The Sexiest Man Alive." In 1990, he again made the *People* list as one of the world's 50 most beautiful people.

The press has also avidly followed his romances. His first long-term relationship was with Sally Munro, a fellow student he met while studying history at Brown University in Providence, Rhode Island. He and Munro dated for four years before John fell for Christina Haag, a part-time actress and writer, whom he has dated on and off since 1986.

In between those two long-standing relationships, he has been linked to a string of beauties, among them Princess Stephanie of Monaco; singers Madonna and Apollonia, the protégée of rock superstar Prince; and actresses Brooke Shields, Molly Ringwald, Sarah Jessica Parker, and Catherine Oxenberg.

But his most widely reported romance has been with blonde actress Daryl Hannah, who starred as a mermaid in the film *Splash*. Gossip columnists reported the couple first met at a wedding dinner given by John's mother, Jackie, for her sister, Lee Radziwill Ross. Since then, he has been spotted on several occasions squiring Hannah around New York City. When Hannah came down with a fever while filming a new movie in Brazil, John reportedly sent 1,000 red roses to her hospital room to cheer her up.

Handsome and charming, John F. Kennedy, Jr., (top) has played the field with a string of beauties: Sally Munro (above, left), Daryl Hannah (above, right), and Princess Stephanie of Monaco (right).

Three Tries at the Bar Exam

By 1989, John had graduated from New York University School of Law and was working as an assistant in the Manhattan district attorney's office at a salary of $30,000 per year.

When he failed his first bar exam in July of that year, the *New York Post* trumpeted the news across the front page in a banner headline that read "The Hunk Flunks." John's embarrassment was compounded by the fact that his sister, Caroline, passed the bar on her first try (which earned her a ten-line mention in the newspaper's gossip column).

John failed again a year later. He had one last chance to pass the bar or lose his job as an assistant prosecutor. Fearing he would again fail in New York, John took the Connecticut bar exam and passed easily. A short time later, he learned he had also passed the bar in New York. He was named to a permanent position with the district attorney's office.

The press's gloating upon John's failure to pass the bar exam (above, left) was embarrassing to him. His sister, Caroline (above, right), passed the bar on her first try. Both of JFK's children have been at times the obsessive focus of demented individuals, including several who came close to killing them. Fear that the worst would happen became a factor in their mother's decision to marry Onassis—the only man in the world who could provide Jackie and her children with the kind of security they needed.

A Kidnapping and Murder Plot

Jackie had long protected her children from the influences of their more wayward cousins, but that protection was not enough to guard against the more bizarre encounters with fate.

One of those occurred in 1972. According to news service reports at the time, a gang of eight Greeks and four West Germans hatched a plot to kidnap 11-year-old John and hold him for ransom. The plot was foiled when Greek authorities arrested the 12 terrorists.

Caroline came close to a tragic encounter in October 1975, when she narrowly escaped death at the hands of militant Irish Republican Army members who had planted a bomb in a car belonging to Hugh Fraser, a member of the British Parliament. The bomb, believed to have been intended for Fraser, exploded moments before he was to drive her to school at London's Sotheby Parke Bernet auction house, where she was attending art classes.

Six years later, in 1981, Caroline became the focus of an obsessed California lawyer intent on winning her hand in marriage. He wrote her scores of threatening and obscene letters and repeatedly attempted to break into her New York apartment. Kevin King, a wealthy, 35-year-old California lawyer, was arrested and convicted of criminal trespass and aggravated harassment. During his trial, King withdrew his marriage offer and then changed his mind, saying his proposal still stood. He was sentenced to a year in jail and fined $1,000 for stalking the former president's daughter.

In 1984, when Caroline was working at the Metropolitan Museum of Art in New York, she was stalked by a former mental patient who threatened her with death at the hands of "20 hitmen." Police later arrested the man, identified as 32-year-old Randall Gefvert, after he phoned the Metropolitan and threatened to blow up the museum.

TED KENNEDY IN MIDDLE AGE

The Playboy of the Senate

His skirt-chasing is legendary in Washington circles.

Struck down in their youth, Ted's three older brothers remain in memory forever in their prime, young and handsome. Ted, however, grew into a seasoned, middle-aged politician. His once ruddy complexion is today creased, his face puffy, his hair silver, but he retains his power on Capitol Hill.

Since divorcing Joan, his wife of 24 years, in 1982, Teddy has become known more for his sexual exploits than his senatorial efforts. His skirt-chasing is legendary in Washington circles. Among reporters who cover the Senate, he is well known for sending younger staffers on "scouting expeditions" to pick up attractive young blondes for his later enjoyment.

His behavior in recent years also has drawn some scandalous publicity. One such incident, documented in *The Washington Times,* occurred in December 1985 at Washington's La Brasserie restaurant, one of the senator's favorite haunts.

According to several witnesses, Teddy and Senator Christopher Dodd of Connecticut were dining with two young women when Teddy allegedly manhandled an attractive young waitress. According to one version of the incident, which appeared in *Penthouse,* a drunken Teddy grabbed the waitress, threw her on top of Dodd and began rubbing his genital area against hers. In the foray, glasses and a candlestick were broken.

Alerted by the noise of breaking glass, restaurant workers ran to the woman's aid. The senator made light of the incident, telling restaurant managers it was only a joke. "Makes you wonder about the leaders of this country," he reportedly said.

Nearly two years after that scene, Teddy again raised eyebrows at La Brasserie. According to a scathing February 1990 article in *Gentleman's Quarterly,* Teddy was lunching with a young woman lobbyist in a private room. The senator's libido, fueled by two bottles of Chardonnay, got out of control. One waitress who heard about the incident told the magazine that Teddy was caught with his pants down— and the woman's dress up—engaging in sex under a table on the carpeted floor.

During a late-night dinner in 1985 at Washington's La Colline restaurant, Teddy allegedly took a photograph of his drinking buddy, Senator Dodd, from the wall and smashed it on the floor. The *Washing-*

tonian magazine, which first reported the incident, said Dodd retaliated good-naturedly by smashing Teddy's photo, doing what one witness called "a Mexican hat dance" on top of it.

In 1989, Teddy's antics made newspapers nationwide when he got into a fight with an ex-cop at the singles bar American Trash in Manhattan. A spokesman for the senator said the fight began after a bar patron "insulted the memory of his brothers." In interviews, however, the ex-cop, Dennis McKenna, said he told the senator, "You're nothing like your other two brothers," and Teddy retaliated by throwing a drink in his face.

The senator has not commented on any of the incidents. Aides at his Washington office said his policy is not to comment on gossip or speculation.

Rumors have linked Ted Kennedy with Angie Dickinson (top). His political life has suffered little from his renowned personal exploits (above).

The Senator's Women

After Ted's Chappaquiddick accident, it was not his wife that he phoned first, but his love interest of the time, former German airline stewardess Helga Wagner. Since that time, Teddy's list of lovelies has included blondes and brunettes, socialites and working girls—many of them known, even more of them unknown. Among them have been skier Suzie Chaffee, Washington socialite Lacey Neuhaus, and longtime love Cindy Pease, a former T-shirt salesgirl with whom he reportedly shared his Washington home.

He has cavorted with actress Angie Dickinson, who was rumored to be a love interest of his brother Jack; dated author and actress Beverly Sassoon, the ex-wife of celebrity hairdresser Vidal Sassoon; and squired dark-haired Texas beauty Charlotte Brewer, the vice president of marketing for a Boston department store.

He also has been known to keep company with actress Cynthia Sykes, a runner-up in the 1972 Miss America pageant who later starred in the TV drama *St. Elsewhere.*

Recently he has been dating raven-haired Stephanie Pinol of Virginia, a 22-year-old college student who is 37 years his junior. A photograph of Teddy and Pinol locked in an obviously compromising position on a speedboat off St. Tropez made the rounds in supermarket tabloids in 1990, causing the senator some personal and political embarrassment.

He was barely over the fallout from that incident when his relationship with a Palm Beach neighbor, Dragana Lickle, became an issue in Lickle's 1991 custody battle with her ex-husband. An attorney for Garrison duPont Lickle, who divorced his wife in 1984 and is now trying to win custody of their two children, said he wanted Teddy to testify at the custody hearing about the places he and Dragana took the children.

In interviews about the case, attorney Joseph Farish claims Dragana has exposed the children to "the lifestyle of the jet set [and] to notorious characters, some of whom have criminal backgrounds and others of questionable character." Fortunately for Teddy, a judge cancelled the testimony, ruling that the senator had been improperly subpoenaed.

THE PALM BEACH SCANDAL

The Kennedy family's palatial compound in Palm Beach, where a woman claims she was raped by William Kennedy Smith on Easter weekend in 1991. In the foreground is the stairway where the woman says she was first attacked by Smith. The woman says he pursued her across the front lawn before raping her near the swimming pool at the left of the picture.

Easter Weekend

She said in a statement to police shortly after the incident that Smith tried to convince her she wasn't raped, telling her, "No one's gonna believe you."

The story of Easter weekend in 1991 spotlights the Kennedy family in another situation involving questionable judgment, fast living, and the possibility of less than full candor with authorities.

Senator Ted Kennedy and his son, Patrick, were staying at the Kennedy family estate with Ted's sister Jean Kennedy Smith and two of her children, Willie and Amanda. Also staying at the estate were William Barry and his family. William Barry was a Kennedy family friend and former FBI agent.

On Good Friday, an attractive, 29-year-old woman, out for a night on the town, dropped in at a swank, ultrachic night spot called Au Bar—the kind of place frequented by the likes of Ivana Trump and Roxanne Pulitzer. In the same night spot, Senator Kennedy, 59, was drinking with 24-year-old son Patrick and 30-year-old Willie Smith.

Willie met the young woman on his way to the restroom. After a few drinks, he invited her back to the Kennedy estate for another drink. That invitation proved to be a costly one for both of them. What developed from it was a charge of sexual assault against Willie and a string of scurrilous accusations against the woman. And despite a longstanding journalism tradition of not revealing the identity of alleged rape victims, the woman has been subjected to seeing her name printed in a number of publications.

The truth of what happened back at the Kennedy mansion is murky at best.

The Woman's Story

According to the woman's account, she was walking with Willie along the beach when he suddenly stripped off his clothes and jumped into the ocean.

Deciding it was time to leave, the woman started walking back to the house. But in a stairway leading up from the beach, soon christened the "Tunnel of Lust" by the tabloids, Willie allegedly grabbed her leg, tackled her, and raped her near an outdoor swimming pool as she screamed for help.

After the alleged attack, the woman returned to the main house to call a friend. She said in a statement to police shortly after the incident that Smith tried to convince her she wasn't raped, telling her, "No one's gonna believe you."

By some accounts, the woman left in her own car and then returned moments later to await the arrival of her friend Anne Mercer and Mercer's boyfriend, Chuck Desiderio. When the couple arrived, Mercer confronted Willie. "How could you do this to her?" she asked.

Frantic and upset, the woman grabbed a photograph of the two children of Willie's cousin Joseph Kennedy and a telephone notepad. Desiderio left the mansion with a decorative urn.

"I thought no one would believe that I'd been raped or that I'd been at that house," the woman explained later. "And I needed something to say that yes, indeed, I had been in that house and I had been raped."

The ultrachic night spot Au Bar (opposite) was hopping on the night William Kennedy Smith (top) and his cousin Patrick Kennedy (left) stopped in with the senator from Massachusetts for a round or two of drinks. During the evening, Smith met the woman who later accused him of rape.

Michele Cassone's Story

Another young woman had met the Kennedys at Au Bar that night. Soon after the incident became public, Palm Beach waitress Michele Cassone began giving out her account of what had occurred on the night of the alleged rape.

Twenty-seven-year-old Michele had met the senator's son, Patrick, at Au Bar that night, and she returned with him to the Kennedy estate for a nightcap. As she sat with Patrick and Teddy on the seawall, listening to the crashing surf and sipping white wine, Michele saw a naked woman with slicked-back hair walk into the ocean. Neither the senator nor his son made any remark about the woman, Cassone recalled. A short while later, things got even more bizarre. Cassone said that as she and Patrick cuddled in a mansion bedroom, Teddy walked through wearing an oxford-cloth shirt and apparently nothing else.

He "was just there with a weird look on his face," Cassone recalled. "I was weirded out."

Disturbed by the night's events, Cassone left the compound. While saying goodbye to Patrick in the compound's parking lot, she noticed another car and a man apparently saying good night to the car's driver. The identity of these two people and also of the naked woman with the slicked-back hair are still unknown.

The Senator's Version

Out of all the depositions taken by investigators probing the alleged rape at the Kennedy compound, Senator Kennedy's is perhaps the most pitiful. According to his sworn testimony, Teddy awakened Patrick and Willie at 11:30 P.M. on Good Friday and asked them to go with him to Au Bar for a nightcap. After drinking several double scotches, Teddy returned home with his son and retired for the evening.

Other witnesses say that the two younger Kennedys hadn't been in bed and had been out at a party, and Ted met up with them at some unspecified time. Michele Cassone's story of seeing Teddy in nothing but an oxford-cloth shirt has also been disputed—he may have changed into a long nightshirt.

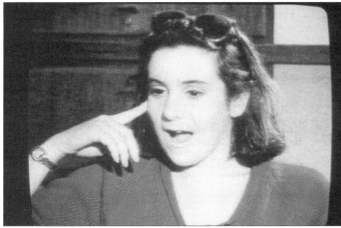

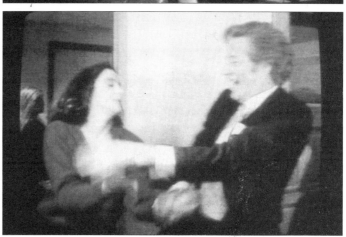

Party girl, waitress, and bakery store heiress Michele Cassone (opposite, top), left Au Bar (opposite, bottom) and went home with Patrick Kennedy. Not long after the Palm Beach story became front-page news, Patrick joined his father for a day of sailing (above) at the Hyannis Port Yacht Club, apparently unbothered by the furor.

Hobnobbing with the Kennedys was glamorous to Michele at the time, but her 15 minutes of fame brought embarrassment to her as well as to the others in the story. She became a media darling with her tintillating story of a pantsless Senator Kennedy prowling the Palm Beach estate. Initially, Michele claimed she would pose for Penthouse magazine dressed in a long oxford-cloth shirt similar to the one she claims Teddy wore.

When confronted about those plans by Steve Dunleavy on Fox-TV's A Current Affair (above), Cassone reneged. No, she said, she would never pose nude. Dunleavy countered by producing a handful of provocative photographs—one (top, left) showing a naked Cassone lounging at a swimming pool. Shocked and angered by the on-air revelation, Cassone railed at Dunleavy, cursing, kicking and biting as she tried to grab the photos from his hands. Michele learned the hard way that life in the limelight has its down side.

In July 1991, three months after her now infamous skirmish with Dunleavy, Cassone was banned from Au Bar for drunken behavior after allegedly shattering a glass door at the Palm Beach club.

By September, Cassone had hit an all-time low. On September 6, she allegedly attempted to kill herself by taking an overdose of sleeping pills. She was hospitalized for the overdose and was later transferred to a mental health facility.

Damage Control

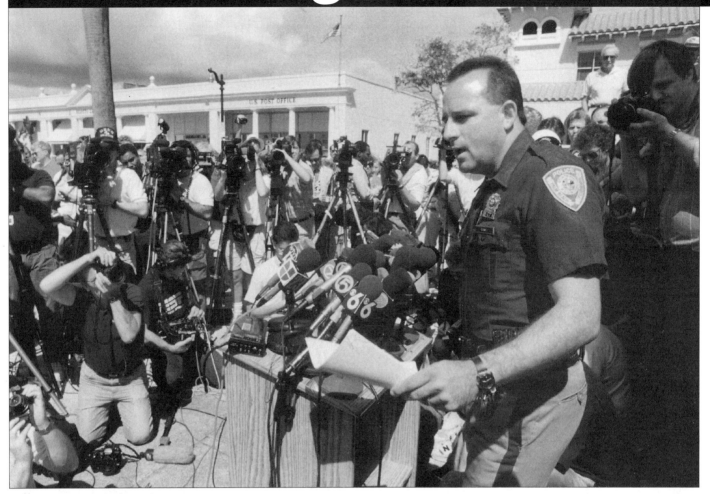

The Kennedys' behavior over the next few days evoked memories of the attempt to control the Chappaquiddick situation more than twenty years before.

On Easter Sunday, a day after the alleged assault, Palm Beach policemen came to the Kennedy compound to question the senator and Willie Smith. William Barry, the former FBI agent who was staying at the compound, let the police believe he was a security guard and informed them neither the senator nor Willie was there. Investigators later learned both Teddy and Willie were lunching at the compound at the time.

By Easter Sunday afternoon, Willie was on a flight to Washington. His uncle Ted and cousin Patrick followed the next day. None of them gave a statement to investigators about what happened that night until a month later.

Despite the intense publicity surrounding the incident, Teddy was belated in giving a statement to police, saying he had been unaware investigators wanted to talk with him. When he finally spoke publicly about the incident, he claimed the police term "sexual battery," Florida's legal term for rape, confused him. He had thought the complaint was merely sexual harassment.

Stymied by the family's lack of cooperation, police were left to interview the Kennedy servants, all of whom denied hearing a woman's screams as she allegedly tried to fight off her attacker.

Then, on April 30, exactly one month after the incident, something strange occurred. A mystery witness—William Barry's son, Patrick—stepped forward to say he had seen two people by the pool on the night in question.

Patrick Barry told investigators he had gotten up to go to the bathroom early March 30 and saw from his window what appeared to be two people lying together on the ground near the estate's swimming pool. It "looked like two people either lying next to each other or, you know, one on top of the other," Barry testified in a sworn statement. Barry said he watched the couple for about ten seconds but heard nothing to suggest that someone was being attacked.

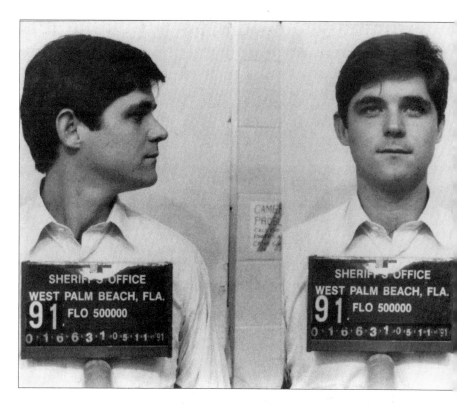

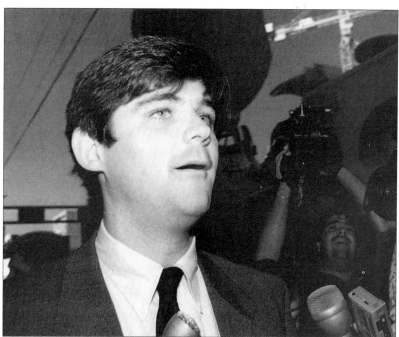

When the police report on the alleged rape at the Kennedy compound was released (opposite, top), it was news throughout the world. Not until 40 days later did police charge William Kennedy Smith with sexual battery in connection with the incident. Two days after he was charged, Smith (opposite, bottom) turned himself in to authorities and was released on bail. Willie Smith, suspect 016631, as he looked in police mug shots (top) following his May 11, 1991, arrest and later (above) as he leaves a hearing at the Palm Beach County Court House. In typical Kennedy style, the clan managed to keep police at bay for days following the alleged Easter weekend attack. It took authorities weeks before they were able to interview the principals in the case.

A Dirty Legal Fight

The question is whether the Palm Beach incident is the final tawdry story to dispel the glow of Camelot.

On May 9, 40 days after the Easter weekend incident, Florida police charged Willie with sexual battery.

Soon, the legal battle lines were being drawn up in the case. On the defense's side was Palm Beach attorney Mark Schnapp, a formidable foe to prosecutor Moira Lasch, the assistant Palm Beach County State's Attorney. Advising Willie in the case was Herbert "Jack" Miller, the Kennedy family lawyer who also advised Teddy after his 1969 car accident at Chappaquiddick.

Stories about the woman's background began appearing in the press—that she was an unmarried mother, that she had numerous traffic violations, that her stepfather was a very wealthy man with a longstanding feud against the Kennedy family. The defense hired private investigators to dig up information on the woman's past sexual conduct.

But Willie's past sexual conduct was also being held up to the light. In July 1991, prosecutor Lasch vowed to produce three women who claimed they also had been attacked by Willie and would testify against Willie in the trial. According to the prosecution documents, Willie Smith allegedly raped one woman at his Washington townhouse in May 1988 after a post-exam party. Another woman claimed Willie had attempted to rape her in the spring of that same year. A third said she had been a victim of an attempted attack in New York City in the summer of 1983.

Florida's State's Attorney announced to the press on May 9, 1991 (above), that he had charged Willie Smith with sexual battery in connection with the alleged Easter weekend rape of a Florida woman.

In the face of these revelations, defense lawyers asked to have the trial delayed and also requested a change in venue. They also requested records of psychological or psychiatric treatment of the alleged victim. The information, Willie's lawyers argued, would show that the woman's past unpleasant experiences with men led her to file false rape charges against their client after consenting to have sex with him. Among those experiences, the defense claimed, were three abortions and a series of failed relationships with men.

Unsavory features in the reputations of both the alleged victim and the accused attacker may come to light in the trial, which is now scheduled for late 1991. The incident has been an enduring subject not only in the supermarket tabloids but in more upscale publications as well. Publicity surrounding the case is also affecting Senator Kennedy, even though he is not involved in the alleged rape. At the least, his sense of propriety and his taste has been questioned: He went out drinking with his young son and nephew on Good Friday, while they picked up women and took the women back to the house. Further, his escape from official questioning the Sunday following the incident produces the impression of another cover-up, another attempt by a powerful family to smooth things over.

Ever since Joe Kennedy's time, the family has been the subject of tawdry stories, innuendoes, and gossip. Even so, the Kennedys became the most prominent family in America, the closest Americans had to a royal family. They have survived three generations of scandal. The question is whether the Palm Beach incident is the final tawdry story to dispel the glow of Camelot. A few months after the incident, *The Boston Herald* and WCVB-TV jointly ran a poll asking about Teddy's future political chances. Respondents overwhelmingly said they preferred to see "someone new" fill the senator's seat in the next election.

Willie Smith's defense lawyer, Mark Schnapp, and legal aide David Chase (above) *outside the Palm Beach County Court House last June after Judge Mary Lupo granted them a continuance.*

Prosecutor Moira Lasch (above) *upped the stakes by threatening to produce three women who would claim they were also attacked by Smith.*

Kennedy Family Tree

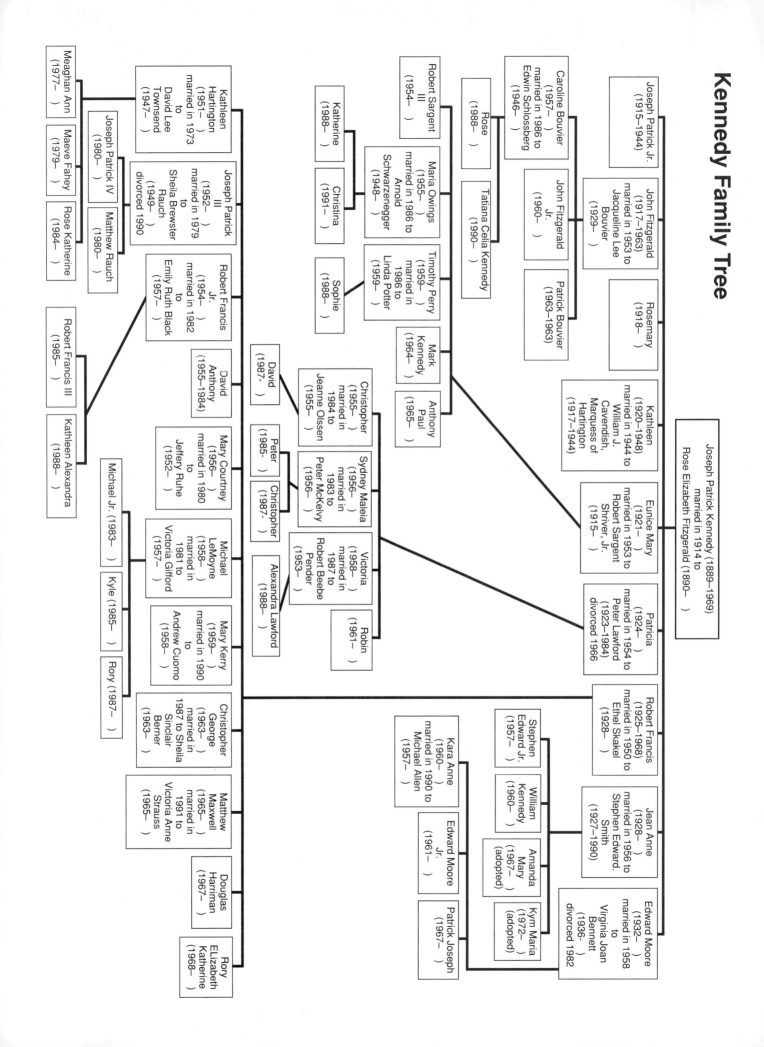

Joseph Patrick Kennedy (1889–1969)
married in 1914 to
Rose Elizabeth Fitzgerald (1890–)

Joseph Patrick Kennedy Jr. (1915–1944)

John Fitzgerald (1917–1963) married in 1953 to Jacqueline Lee Bouvier (1929–)
- Caroline Bouvier (1957–) married in 1986 to Edwin Schlossberg (1946–)
  - Rose (1988–)
  - Tatiana Celia Kennedy (1990–)
- John Fitzgerald Jr. (1960–)
- Patrick Bouvier (1963–1963)

Rosemary (1918–)

Kathleen (1920–1948) married in 1944 to William J. Cavendish, Marquess of Hartington (1917–1944)

Eunice Mary (1921–) married in 1953 to Robert Sargent Shriver, Jr. (1915–)
- Robert Sargent III (1954–)
- Maria Owings (1955–) married in 1986 to Arnold Schwarzenegger (1948–)
  - Katherine (1988–)
  - Christina (1991–)
- Timothy Perry (1959–) married in 1986 to Linda Potter (1959–)
  - Sophie (1988–)
- Mark Kennedy (1964–)
- Anthony Paul (1965–)

Patricia (1924–) married in 1954 to Peter Lawford (1923–1984) divorced 1966
- Christopher (1955–) married in 1984 to Jeanne Olssen (1955–)
  - David (1987–)
- Sydney Maleia (1956–) married in 1983 to Peter McKelvy (1956–)
  - Peter (1985–)
  - Christopher (1987–)
- Victoria (1958–) married in 1987 to Robert Beebe Pender (1953–)
  - Alexandra Lawford (1988–)
- Robin (1961–)

Robert Francis (1925–1968) married in 1950 to Ethel Skakel (1928–)
- Kathleen Hartington (1951–) married in 1973 to David Lee Townsend (1947–)
  - Meaghan Ann (1977–)
  - Maeve Fahey (1979–)
  - Rose Katherine (1984–)
- Joseph Patrick III (1952–) married in 1979 to Sheila Brewster Rauch (1949–) divorced 1990
  - Joseph Patrick IV (1980–)
  - Matthew Rauch (1980–)
- Robert Francis Jr. (1954–) married in 1982 to Emily Ruth Black (1957–)
  - Robert Francis III (1985–)
  - Kathleen Alexandra (1988–)
- David Anthony (1955–1984)
- Mary Courtney (1956–) married in 1980 to Jeffery Ruhe (1952–)
- Michael LeMoyne (1958–) married in 1981 to Victoria Gifford (1957–)
  - Michael Jr. (1983–)
  - Kyle (1985–)
  - Rory (1987–)
- Mary Kerry (1959–) married in 1990 to Andrew Cuomo (1958–)
- Christopher George (1963–) married in 1987 to Sheila Sinclair Berner (1963–)
- Matthew Maxwell (1965–) married in 1991 to Victoria Anne Strauss (1965–)
- Douglas Harriman (1967–)
- Rory Elizabeth Katherine (1968–)

Jean Anne (1928–) married in 1956 to Stephen Edward. Smith (1927–1990)
- Stephen Edward Jr. (1957–)
- William Kennedy (1960–)
- Amanda Mary (1967–) (adopted)
- Kym Maria (1972–) (adopted)

Edward Moore (1932–) married in 1958 to Virginia Joan Bennett (1936–) divorced 1982
- Kara Anne (1960–) married in 1990 to Michael Allen (1957–)
- Edward Moore Jr. (1961–)
- Patrick Joseph (1967–)